More than a Bit Black

Memoir of a Black Woman's Child

A. CENTAURI

13TH & JOAN

For permission requests, write to the publisher, addressed "Attention: Permissions Coordinator," 205 N. Michigan Avenue, Suite #810, Chicago, IL 60601. 13th & Joan books may be purchased for educational, business or sales promotional use. For information, please email the Sales Department at sales@13thandjoan.com.

Printed in the U. S. A.

First Printing, March 2023.

Library of Congress Cataloging-in-Publication Data has been applied for.

ISBN: 978-1-7322479-9-4

DEDICATION

I dedicate this book to single black moms and praying
grandmothers like mine. Thank you for your sacrifice.
You are appreciated. You birthed greatness.

To my Momma and Gramma,

You both instilled in me to gift people flowers while they're alive and always say thank you. I have peace because I was sure to do that for you.

I was also taught to lead by example. Hopefully, this book does just that. I pray that it leads its readers straight to Jesus. "The best gift you could ever give to me".

— Ahsh

"In every human Breast, God has implanted
a Principle, which we call Love of Freedom;
it is impatient of Oppression, and pants
for Deliverance."

— Phillis Wheatley, 1774

TABLE OF CONTENTS

LETTER FROM AUTHOR

I **REMEMBER WHEN I** fell in love with words. It was summer and I was waiting for the first day of 4th grade down in the country. My grandmother was in the living room seated in her chair, the front door wide open, the screen door bolted shut, AM radio playing as the condensation from her glass of Sprite left a ring on the old wooden table.

I was comfy sitting crisscross applesauce in my grandma's favorite sleeping spot at the right-side edge of her old king-sized bed; purple Mead journal opened, so my pencil danced. I wrote so much that day, the pencil went dull and I watched my Uncle use a cooking knife to sharpen it.

I'd spent every day that summer writing about everything I could think of. There was no point sharing them with my grandma, I could write my name 100x and she'd have loved it. So I'd wait until my mom was done teaching summer school and share them all with her. She would listen intently to the phone and ask questions, encouraging me to "edit it then edit some more".

I would compete with myself to see if I could write something more fascinatingly prolific than the last. Using my mother as the tiebreaker, aiming for a bigger response than the one I'd gotten from her previously.

The first time my grandma took me to the public library was that same summer. I told my mom that I wanted my writing to get better and she suggested I read more. Having read all the books and Jet Magazines that were available at my grandmother's house, she told me to ask my grandma to take me to the library. The next morning my grandmother and I had breakfast, got dressed and my Uncle took us downtown Barnesville in his red Ford Ranger. We were going to the library.

I remember the feeling of writing my name on the back of the card, careful not to smudge the ink. I hope I never forget the way the long cold brass handle felt against my back as I pressed into it to open the door to leave. My hands stacked so full of books I couldn't see the door to use the handles. I ended up going to the library so often my Uncle grew tired of taking me. My grandma always made sure he did though, no matter what.

I've had a tumultuous love affair with reading and writing ever since. Whether it's term papers, love notes, or a collection of poems, short stories, and truths that you're reading right now. No matter the reason behind the writing, if it was written for a release, or an assignment; I love words and how they work together. I love the feeling I get combining them to communicate. I hope this comes across in my work and that you enjoy reading this as much as I have writing it for you.

— A.

A GENESIS STORY

Ask me,
The Black Woman
Is America's success story.

Do you disagree?
Think differently?
Why?

Because "white is right" and men are kings,
European
men
And their
descendants, that is

what you've been taught to think.

Since you're asking me...
As you read this black ink that bleeds into this white page,
    perspective will be gained.

For there are 5 sides to American History.
It is deep
and heavy, long
cyclical.

GOD is the creator of us all.
Ready for the story?

OUR BEINGS—HUMAN BEINGS—LIKE Jesus, journey to America on a boat. I am choosing to leave out all the gruesome details of the actual trip that we all know (whether we acknowledge it or not) for chronological reasons and time sake. So, four beings are on a boat. All of them are some nuanced shade of yellow or brown. Half of the occupants are sticks, and the other half bleed. This means nothing until it turns into everything.

Power. The fifth occupant neither sticks nor bleeds. It simply exists. Although power is on the boat, it has no form, no mass, no face. It is only energy.

Energy when conceptualized may act as currency.

Power—is the strongest entity on the boat. The body (bleed, stick, dark brown, or pale yellow) that possessed it won the next 8 centuries.

History was re-written.

Africa lost.

I was 25 years old when I realized everything I ever knew was a lie. I started questioning myself simply because I felt as if who I was had all been designed and crafted by something else and I was actually nothing. I found myself spiraling into a depression, so I dedicated myself to not strapping in and leaning into it. For the first time, I felt empowered even though gravity was forcefully pressing down.

Mother passed on. Grandmother passed on. Father no longer obligated to participate, therefore *absent* and I was the most joyful I had ever been. I was in a stable relationship with a healthy man, even though we disagreed on quite a lot, at first. I fell in love because he was sure to stay and listen for the solution, no matter the disagreement. My friendships were falling apart, but the Lord was speaking to me and I was being still to listen. I delight in listening, still. (I think that's how you train yourself to discern.) Anyhow, this was the battle my mother trained me for my entire life. I had to perform, design, construct, sustain, and maximize. It was showtime. Thank GOD for Jesus.

At 22, I was blessed to have my mother watch me take a vow to serve the Lord in the name of his sacrifice, Jesus. She was alive to take pictures of me in white after being baptized. She was strong to stand up without the confines of an oxygen tank and record my purging of past debts/relationships and the cleansing of my spirit. She would later find herself lovingly overjoyed as she cheered me across the Kennesaw State University stage to accept my degree. She did it, and she got me through. She raised her child.

I was 23 when she passed away from undetected breast cancer that traveled to her lungs. The lesson in that? If they find a lump remove the entire breast. She only took out the lump and after chemo, radiation, and 5 years of mammograms, hers came back.

After my mother's passing, life got real. It felt like every second she and I ever spent with each other, every minute she spent fussing, every lesson she ever gave me was all dress rehearsal for my debut Broadway hit, *Life without Mom*. It was weird; in her passing, we are closer than ever.

I could hear her, feel her, and know she was with me. She continues to guide me. I thank GOD for her every day.

I was blessed to ensure that my mother was at peace. The blessing was knowing she was ready to leave. She told me she was ready to die. That gave me three things to do:

1. Trust in GOD's plan for *my* life.
2. Be obedient.
3. ~~survive~~ LIVE.

In losing a parent, the sitcoms and entertainment media will lead you to believe that the world stops and mourns with you. After years of empathizing with movie plots, I thought other people would show compassion and aid in assisting me through "such a difficult time" (words murmured by what felt like everyone). Aside from telling me of their condolences the

Americans I came in contact with were unable to genuinely care. Unbeknownst to me, that was the first red flag; the first sign that the life I believed myself to be living and the one that I am actually a part of are not congruent. It's at this point in my life that I started relating to Bible stories.

I remember vividly reading about Lot and the task he was blessed with. I couldn't imagine at the time what that was like and remember questioning GOD about it. My grandma always warned me to be careful about the things I asked GOD because I'd get the answer and may regret ever asking the question. I don't regret asking, but I have newfound compassion and understanding of empathy. I won't be questioning anymore.

I noticed with my mom's passing; loved ones started changing narratives. I have come to know this as grief. My mother's siblings, aunts, uncles, cousins, nieces, nephews, friends collectively sought comfort in various coping mechanisms that clashed with the way in which I needed support. Unfortunately, in my grief, I took their behavior as blame-shifting and character assassination; I saw them as liars.

I remember never feeling able to breathe because I was trained to be guarded. I held my breath to move in silence and only trusted those I knew. All of which are standard survival tactics used by black Americans in a country that is constantly surveilling, criminalizing, and terrorizing them. Unfortunately, those skills bleed over into the family's dynamic, and many gossip and become distrusting of one another.

I was blessed to have had a mother with foresight; so many things were taken care of as it relates to her passing. I just had to be emotionally mature enough to follow through with the lessons learned fully. Though I had help, I felt as if I was handling everything on my own. That was the second red flag.

The first time it crossed my mind that things were not what they seemed was on the job. I was working at a job that I loved. I really want to emphasize *loved*. I was comfortably content in my given role and had no plans of seeking advancement. I just wanted to do my job; I felt like it was made for me. I thought I cultivated genuine relationships and that my co-workers would be the family I felt I lacked.

Media tells you, "some people throw themselves into work when they're grieving". I thought that would be me. I thought I would be able (after 13 days) to head back to work and do my duties and put everything out of my mind. That worked perfectly until something triggered a depressive state without warning. As soon as I had one "bad" day, my loss became their ammunition to use against me. Within 6 months, I would be coerced into "putting myself first" and resigning from my position. With that resignation went a resignation from my friendships, bonds, and new adjusted lifestyle with my co-workers. I look back on that time and feel the embarrassment and gratitude that I have overcome.

I should have found the irony behind "take as long as you need" and "this is a business, the show must go on" more alarming than I did. Had I realized, I would have asked for personal copies of all the comments made about me by guests— those reviews / references were invaluable—the messenger should not be trusted with personal assets like your credibility.

The biggest red flag came with announcing my mother passed on social media. Half of the people I love and care for were genuinely saddened by the news. A quarter of them did not know her to care at all and the remaining few were tuning in to see if I would end up overdosing on heroin like my live-in ex-boyfriend had done the year before. The flag appeared after I realized high school relationships were more surface-level than deep. I didn't know what I was feeling, but I felt things building up. I would come to learn that I was experiencing an awakening. I was coming to know that I knew nothing.

Everything about the public school system was a scam designed to keep us confined to the imaginary caste system we graduated from. I would become financially indebted even though my mother and I did everything *right*. I had good grades, extracurriculars, and exceptional behavior. I was accepted into every college I applied for. My mother, a hardworking scholar, was untied to government assistance living in the heart of the southern upper-middle class.

We had done everything right. Yet, we felt as though we were being punished. Punished for not falling victim to stereotypes and societal misconceptions about black-skinned people. Ultimately, with her passing, I can now say we felt as if at every turn we were being punished for stepping out of the place *society's dictated.*

I was alone to stand on my own as a woman, I started to become curious about who *they* are and why *they* even put me in a place. I learned *they* are those who make money off the poverty and ignorance of people. This ruling class only knows the rules of the game because their great-grandparents invented it. *They* only know who *they* are because they keep each other's secrets.

They are a closed-off society that believes they know best for the country and its economy. *They* have created gods of men and provoked titans' battles. Destruction of humankind brings immense wealth to their lineage. They decide who is granted permission to have access to the foods we eat, and who should be designated for extermination. They are the media, the corporations, and the derivatives of white men's organizations created at Bretton Woods in 1944.[1]

Understanding who "they" are, reveals why black Americans have felt terrorized in their home country and that the underlying problem is the money system. All of the red flags were actually spiritual trailblazers. I was on a path that was leading me away from the destructive path of the modern world and its financial system down an honest path of truth, work, peace, and Bitcoin. All I ever want to do is follow Jesus. The path is narrow but it's gorgeous and safe.

The father of Black History, Dr. Carter G. Woodson, famously studied and wrote about blackness in post-slavery America. In his book, *The Miseducation of the Negro* covert anti-black tactics are discussed in a way that eerily foreshadows the problems, the anti-black resentments, and lack of upward mobility within the black community today. For example,

---

1   Griffin, G. Edward. "What Creature Is This?" The Creature from Jekyll Island: A Second Look at the Federal Reserve, American Media, Westlake Village, CA, 2010, pp. 3–153.

in the essay Dr. Woodson discusses the downfalls of highly educated negroes; to paraphrase, he argues, that college-educated blacks leave home to attend university only to pursue a job as a "team member" for a white company or corporation. He further argues not returning home with those college learned skills and/or failing to stay home to learn the skill of the family is detrimental to black society.

As the price to attend college continues to soar, black families have undertaken stress that has crippled the health of a once vibrant community. Post-college students either have to take out more debt to further their education or they have to look for a job to climb someone else's ladder. Why are we even climbing a ladder? Is there an easier way to get there that won't cost me my life and my future? There is no ladder. It's jargon originating from cronyism that means nothing in essence. If you want to get to the top— do honest business, be dedicated, and harness your own power to ultimately open your own business, then raise a family that understands the importance of longevity and allows them to build and improve upon the foundation your ownership laid. The key is in the ability to think for yourself.

It is sad to say but a book written 100 years ago predicted black America's demise. Simply by Dr. Woodson observing and understanding how white overseers in America were taking control of the way in which the formerly enslaved blacks of the 1900s were thinking he was able to predict how white America's industry makers were going to usurp black culture. *They* would homogenize it with criminality, and proceed to use the labels created to openly extinguish black people, primarily Black men, at the approval of other prominent blacks. Unfortunately, these blacks have agreed to go along with the given labels simply to enjoy the perks of being an elite "high-level" team member[2].

I remember watching a Netflix documentary called, *The Social Dilemma*. It was a "docu-drama" that masterfully enlightened viewers on the computer science philosophy behind social networks (free social media sites) and the data that comes from them. It's a movie I suggest everyone watch— however, it's not necessary that you have seen it to follow along with the rest of this book. The documentary describes how mathematic algorithms are used. These algorithms dictate who views our content, what content is most popular, what content should be seen by all users, etc. This is done to influence users to make certain purchases, subscribe to certain ideologies, as well as believe in altered realities.

It is nerve-racking how intertwined technology is with our daily lives as human beings. Before the world was locked down we as people were incentivized (to an extent) to take our health in our own hands. We wanted to look good for x-event so we would do something to make sure we presented our best (travel, diet, exercise, shop). We were unafraid to be our best selves and encouraged to show up for ourselves. Post Coronavirus Pandemic, the alternate reality has become the human need for constant connection is only satisfied via social networking. That is because individual health is no longer the

---

2   Woodson, Carter Godwin. The Mis-Education of the Negro. IAP, 2010.

responsibility of the individual but is the responsibility of the public. This shift in thinking causes us to cover our faces, avoid interacting with strangers, hermit away, and gather our human connection through the meta-verse, misjudging free choice for inhuman selfishness and political enemies.

The perfect example can be found in the murder and aftermath of George Floyd. It is understood that most people worldwide found out about his unfortunate murder via social sites as opposed to the reports of the Walter Cronkite from yesteryear. This is an awesome innovation, in a sense that in response, black America and its allies rallied behind one another and demanded some sense of justice. Each individual has the right to do with their time as they see fit. These individuals chose to loudly demonstrate their grief, I respect that. The problems came from the response on social media in its aftermath. Instead of black organizations rallying to force actionable change, white supremacy in blackface was allowed to bait and switch black Americans with propaganda. Viscerally angry blacks and confused poor whites across every socioeconomic strata perpetuated division and tensions that could only live online.

Adults, children, social pundits, and respected leaders were all guilty of Tweeting malicious, hateful, unsubstantiated libel to prove a point to others, a point that may be dangerous to make physically. One of the joys of the internet is how it anonymizes the way we interact with one another. It is our interactions with one another that defines and impacts our humanness. It is how we show empathy and compassion for one another. Dr. Woodson discusses this when looking at "the church's" impact on the formerly enslaved's "thinking". By controlling the way people relate to their emotions the church was able to convince people away from doing neighborly charity and moving towards being subservient to another's moral philosophy.

Unfortunately, this is another example of Dr. Woodson being right. A century later black people are being controlled to think against what is best for themselves. The more you put online, the more famous you become; such an understanding is one I've come to after years of wishing to be famous and realizing why that could never be. Why? The short answer: algorithms.

The honest answer: My momma gave me to Jesus in her womb and that is a love that won't let me connect with idols. The secular answer: My mom raised me to be a free thinker; it is almost impossible for me to give up myself entirely unabashedly to the world online. There is an incongruence between who I was raised to be, what was modeled for me, and what the world deems appropriate. Character is a very strong separating factor.

As a child, I couldn't wait to be a woman; I prayed for time to slow down so I could learn how to make friends and interact with girls and their sisters. I prayed for time to speed up so I could be 16 and go to prom, 18 and go on dates. 21 and have sex at college, and 25 and be "grown- grown". Now that I'm 27, I thank my mother for raising me to be apart. My impatience has also taught me the true value of time.

At 27, I ask myself: why I am still on Social Media? I have my own folly with social networking psychosis. I struggle with an inability to understand the boundary between real-life and faux-real life. Anyhow, as an adult, having seen the social dilemma, I realized for the formative years of my life I was being conditioned by curriculums to be controlled in every way possible. My mom hated social media and she hated my posting. At this time every major argument I had with her felt like she was trying to manipulate and control me. Looking back it's laughable how immature my thinking was.

I lost her at 23. When my mom lived I thought it was the world that wanted me to be free. That was a lie. The world wanted to manipulate and control me because it made the market more profitable. Freedom comes from thinking and finding solutions with the resources you have. Ironic how that lined up with my mother's teachings.

CHAPTER 1

THE FOUNDATION

THE MOTHERLAND OF civilization is Africa. Africa is the world's second-largest continent, geographically. It is the ancestral homeland of God's created people.

In 1877, Lewis Morgan[3], an anthropologist and social theorist, described seven stages that evolutionarily explained the stages of culture. His model was one many theorists, economists, and governments perpetuated as a credible school of thought for centuries. Just like a majority of the 16th, 17th, and 18th-century colonizers and imperialists, Morgan was wrong. His theory only accounted for 5000 years of human life. As we are now in the 21st century, we now know that the ideology concerning linear evolutionary development is wrong.

Morgan argues the lowest status of savagery is denoted from the origin of the human race up until humans learned how to utilize fire. This stage is where most enslaved Africans were believed to have been at the time when the transatlantic slave trade started. This highest status was attributed to the

---

3   Jackson, John G. Introduction to African Civilizations. Citadel Press, 2001.

European Colonialist/empires (who also happened to be the countrymen of Morgan) because they were well read, traveled, written, and spoken.

Archeologist anthropologist and medical professional Dr. Albert Churchward's 20th century findings were discussed in *Fistful of Shell's,* an anthropological work of extensive research on West Africa's gold trade. Dr. Churchward reports the earliest evidence of members in the human species appeared in Central Africa almost 3 million years ago[4]. He furthers his argument by saying the first humans were from Africa's great lakes region. Groups of these people wandered the Nile Valley Region settling in Egypt then spread throughout the entire world. These people would go on to domesticate animals, excel in hunting, trade, and war.

Professor Charles Hapgood, in his publishing titled *Maps of the Ancient Sea Kings* states "We shall now assume that some 20,000 or more years ago, while Paleolithic people held out in Europe more advanced cultures existed elsewhere on earth." Most history argues that Europeans advanced at a higher rate than Africans. That school of thought justified the inhuman treatment of African people during imperialism/colonization. Hapgood's conclusions change the narrative that has been perpetuated for centuries. Hapgood's findings further detail how black Americans, the direct ancestors of stolen African bodies, are still being miseducated.

---

4   Green, Toby. A Fistful of Shells: West Africa From the Rise of The Slave Trade to the Age of Revolution. Allen Lane / Penguin History, 2019.

Hapgood's argument furthers the argument that Africa is the region of origin for humanity. With that understanding, it's important that we discuss the home of Blackness and black terror in detail. As my grandmomma used to tell me, "once you know who you are and where you come from, you can decide where you want to go." We are heading to a road of independence.

Unfortunately, as Black Americans, too much of what we know is about our living in bondage and coping with it. Though slavery is an important part of blackness and the black experience, the frequent dialogue often leaves us feeling broken, belittled, and hopeless. We are heading to a place of independence so we must now be empowered by our past in its entirety. A detailed look at our past before and after the expansion of the Western world leads us to a greater understanding of what blackness is.

Who are black people? And why is blackness unique only to those who are descendants of the enslaved? These answers will help us understand why we deserve to be empowered to do better and have more for ourselves. Especially knowing the ones who defined and justified the enslavement of our ancestral people.

The best example of this can be found in the writing of Lewis Henry Morgan; ironically in his work *Ancient Society*, he argues barbarianism was evacuated with the introduction of the Iron Age. He suggests civilized beings (Europeans) were the ones who cultivated iron ore. Unfortunately, there have been findings since the time of Morgan suggesting that the

Iron Ages started in the area most ravaged by the European monarchs on a plight to pull their way out of poverty from the Middle Ages. It is later revealed that Western Africans were the originators of iron smelting before any other people. [5]

Before Africa could be considered "third world" it was the originator to the first civilizations. I type this with strength and a profound understanding of why my mother took pride in choosing a father for me from Africa and spent so long ensuring I knew what it meant to be both, African and Black American.

I also understand why this knowledge had to be hidden from its broken ancestry. It is dangerous to the founding financiers for black Americans and post-colonial Africans to know the truth of their lineage. I also understand why those who lack the ability to take responsibility for the mistreatment of the past, must hide behind fake narratives in the present. The truth is too damaging and much kinder when left in the past. It's easier to discuss and pretend to correct. Unfortunately, not talking about it dooms us to perish from ignorance; it can be witnessed in black American history, economic history, and familial histories as well.

Ancient Africans were called "the tallest, most beautiful, most long-living" by Herodotus, the father of history. Homer, author of the epic *Odyssey* and *Illiad* called African people

---

5   Jackson, John G. Introduction to African Civilizations. Citadel Press, 2001.

the "most just and favored amongst the gods."[6] Before blacks were slaves, black-skinned people were revered and highly respected. We were seen as otherworldly, peaceful, and strong. It was not written of us as criminal, savage, or sexually provocative until after the introduction of American Slavery.

GOLD. TRADE.

Trade is as essential to human interaction as breathing. People of different regions throughout the world set up markets along popular travel routes and geographic borders that allowed spices, technology, culture, religion, and art amongst other goods and services to be exchanged for items not found in the trader's region. It was along trade routes that educators, historians, and philosophers met to have discussions and learn from one another. Historians of the west perpetuated a false narrative of African trade for centuries that minimized the continent's contribution to global intelligence.

It is often misunderstood that Africans of antiquity lack a monetary (economic) history. Africans living on the shores of the Atlantic Ocean knew the importance of free trade because they understood the mechanics of competition amongst other empires along the same coastline. Discussions of African contribution are often convoluted with the conversation of the transatlantic slave trade and the morality of humans as livestock. Africans have a history prior to the age of European

---

6   Jackson, John G. Introduction to African Civilizations. Citadel Press, 2001.

"exploration". In 1324, Mansa Musa of the Mali Empire would become one of world history's wealthiest humans. His pilgrimage to Mecca and its grandeur would be spoken of for millennia after his death and his empire's.

America's Public Education system's history books propagate Ancient Africans as savage people with elementary bartering techniques. America's children are taught Ancient Africans learned how to trade by interacting with Europeans. American curriculums suggest Africans were so underdeveloped in trading that their lack of self-control led them to sell themselves into slavery.

I'm often tortured with the memory of a friend's mother reminding me that Africans "traded" each other for alcohol, ammunition, and the white man's approval. Her ignorance perplexed me into a paranoia where I began to beg to be the exception. I was gonna be "black, but not like *black*". I was 9 and went from wanting to be like Janet Jackson to wanting to be like Hilary Clinton despite my mother's urging to "be myself".

The public education system creates slavery apologists. Its curriculum is based on pacifying the emotional discourse that discussions of the economic foundation of our nation stir. Unfortunately, this peaceful suggestion yields omissions of truths that are disruptive to the biological speciation of animals with different genes of the same species.

During the European Dark Ages (453 AD-1450 AD), Africa was developing a strong Gold Trade. Northern Africa, Egypt, West Africa, and Eastern Africa were all growing massive economic infrastructures around resources that were abundant to them.

They believed to be led by the spirits of nature and therefore were prosperous in their iron, timber, and ivory work. The ancient African understanding of astronomy developed units of measurement deemed standard to the global sciences.

When black Americans' ancestors walked the earth, they utilized resources in ways that allowed for longevity and familial succession. Each individual had a role to play in daily life, each individual subscribed to improving society however their skills best permitted. Individuals would band together and form villages with dynamic political infrastructure predating that of America's colonizers. Neighboring villages would work together and share geographic boundaries with the common respect for the creator of all things and the spirit of nature. Their skills and use of resources enabled trade with neighboring villages. The land in every aspect was (and in someplace still is) sacred. Anthropologist author Toby Green in his book, *A Fist Full of Shells*, discusses how African spirituality aided African empires in taking control of the gold trade in the 12-15th centuries.

West African gold miners used the spirit and energy of the land to tell them where to mine, it also shaped their work schedule. West African gold enabled the empires of the Mediterranean to expand their understanding of the world. Gold was so abundant in West Africa modern economic historians believe it was overproduced. Therefore, when Africans went to trade gold for textiles and other goods along the trade routes, it yielded bitter jealousy and exploitation.

It's funny to think of gold being overproduced today. In the twenty-first century, gold is still a commodity however, with each passing day it is losing its footing as it relates to Bitcoin. In the time before Bitcoin, the internet, the lightbulb, and the printing press—there was gold. It lived beneath the ground but was also salting the sandy beaches of Namibia. Unfortunately, as African travelers traveled outside of their gold-producing wonderland and explored north of the Mediterranean, they saw gold was seen as a prized commodity in Europe especially. While Africans had abundant growing land and gold Europeans were cheaply producing aluminum, steel, and alcohol in mass quantities; Europe was poor.

Everything in life is dependent on value not being intrinsic. My mother used to tell me "beauty is in the eye of the beholder and pretty is a dime a dozen". In high school, I thought the saying was about building my character and not focusing on being too ugly for the boys to ask out. When I jumped down Bitcoin's rabbit hole, I understood she was discussing value. There is no universal "pretty" because a being's value of beauty depends on the being's personal needs, wants, and desires.[7]

That same understanding can be had with money. The combination of a being's need, resources, and geographic region dictates what is valuable. It has not been until Bitcoin that the world has a currency that equally benefits all of its users.

---

7   Green, Toby. A Fistful of Shells: West Africa From the Rise of The Slave Trade to the Age of Revolution. Allen Lane / Penguin History, 2019.

SLAVERY

I've come to understand that there are 4 forms of slavery: Ancient, American, Post-Modern, and Psychological.

• Ancient Slavery is the slaving practice of the pre-westernized world. In America's "Bible Belt" this is considered the practice of the Old Testament. These were instances in which physical indebtedness came about via war, birth, abandonment, or punishment. Different people around the world approached the practices differently. There was no one common understanding of the manner in which slavery was permitted. The religious beliefs of different geographic collective groups dictated the intensity of the slaves' treatment. For example, Ancient Roman slaves were treated harshly. They were considered property and their lives were dispensable to their owner. This is a sharp contrast to the way Ancient African rulers of the Sahel's understood slavery. During the pilgrimage from Mali, Emperor Mansa Musa endowed each of his slaves with a gold staff for the journey across the Sahara Desert to Mecca. The slaving practices of other African Empires are very similar to the understanding shared with the Israelites of the Bible. The slave was not a person to be dominated but an essential element of upper/upper-middle-class life where the family could afford a live-in Nanny/housekeeper. The slaves were still their own individuals.

In this environment, the penalty for murdering a slave was death.

- American Slavery is a concept of slavery the world has come to see as horrid. It is the worst thing to have happened in Western/Global history. It is so bad that most are so horrified by it that they choose to ignore it and avoid any conversation or reminder of it. In looking at the Holocaust, an equally atrocious time period of global history, the world is not allowed to forget, for there are memorials, monuments, movies, and diaries acting as constant reminders. American slavery has left such a scar that discussions are often overpowered by the Civil War, its characters, and the Emancipation Proclamation. This form of slavery is based on the Holy Roman slavery of the past. It is the form of slavery that brought empires so much earthly riches that it became protected by the United States of America in its fight for independence. It was upheld and enforced by the United States Supreme Court. The interconnectedness of the church, state, and American economy perpetuated American slavery to last for millennia. This form of slavery gave rise to the divisive concept of *race* a term dictating the group of people excluded from the competition of Global financial domination. The construction of *race* has impacted society in such a way that *race* in the 21st century acts as market indicators and manipulators. People subscribe to specific *races* without understanding the etymology of the word further minimizing the chances any civilian wants to have a civilized discussion about the *race's* starting line. It is important to note, the physicality of American Slavery ended with the American Civil War; however, the concept was transformed and upheld by the Supreme Court of the United Stated via Jim Crow laws of segregation (EX: separate but equal yet black Americans received unequal treatment), Civil Rights Laws of 1964 (EX: exclusionary practices in the banking and housing markets), and the Patriot Act of 2004 (law enforcement given the right to stop and search without a warrant).

- Post-Modern Slavery is the slavery that is still currently plaguing the world. Colloquially discussed as Human Trafficking, Post-Modern Slavery is a consummation of the Internet age and corrupt global financial market. Post-modern Slavists view human beings as commodities. Global powers hold a monopoly on violence. This hold on violence means they profit from violence at every cost. This incentivizes people to sell themselves, their children, or violently/forcefully smuggle other human beings as a source of revenue for themselves or their organization.

- Psychological Slavery is the mental enslavement of humans that presume themselves free. This can be practiced peer to peer; however, this form of captivity is primarily practiced by governments via propaganda and politics. This form of slavery victimizes the taxpayers, voters, and asylum seekers. This form of slavery promotes life as a facade where choices are privileges given to the elite to disperse amongst the masses. This torture steals human time, talents, and resources while portraying false truths and misunderstandings as common facts. Victims choose to think alongside the elite as opposed to relying on research or free thought.

It is important to differentiate between the types of slavery when discussing slavery and its higher-order consequences on Black, African-American, and Afro-Caribbean people. Present-day black Americans are directly impacted by this miscommunication in every aspect of life, especially work and/ or political life. Until 2021, a stance on Slavery was assumed by the color an American voted for which in-coincidentally is the same color defining gerrymandered districts. Redlining is a thoroughly discussed practice that Isaiah Jackson discusses in *Bitcoin and Black America (v1 and v2)*. It will not be a topic of discussion here.

RELIGION

Before Noah built the ark, the world was one large landmass. Earth's human inhabitants lived and worshiped a variety of gods. Creation myths often shed light on the metaphysical relationship ancient civilizations shared with the world they were living in. Most were polytheists who acknowledged and worshipped heaven's fallen angels.

The great flood would bring forth a resurfacing of the earth that would destroy the bad and restore the good. Consequential to the flood the earth would no longer be connected as one big landmass. There would also be a shift in philosophical understanding leading away from polytheism, moving towards monotheism. Monotheism, the belief in one God, would be introduced unto the world by a variety of prophets, priests, disciples, and with the teachings and life of an earthly born sacrificial messiah, Jesus.

In GOD's creation and resurfacing of the earth; humans were blessed to experience GOD's love through the bounty and abundance of the earth's resources. Any resource needed to sustain life would be present. As the world evolved into its early stages of globalization, gold became consecrated and coveted. Its earliest times enabled empire building and vast riches. It also created markets of mass exploitation.

Religion, the belief in and worship of some controlling superhuman power, was key to understanding the majesty of the geographic region early humans experienced daily. Religion fueled exploration kept believers feeling safe. In dynastic lineages, religion dictates the ruler of the land connecting religion and government.

The greatest example of this connection is found in Islam. A monotheistic religion that respects piety, faithfulness, giving unto the poor, and ultimately, the belief in one God. Mohammad El Amin Abdullah, Islam's instituter, was a pious man who isolated himself away from the immorality and polytheism of his clansmen and peers. Even the Christian rulers over the land were materialistic and oppressive. Assassination attempts would force Mohammed on a 300-mile journey out of his homelands.

Mohammed would prove to be a valiant general when he and his religious companions were forced away from their homeland and forced into Jewish territory. Judaism, another monotheistic religion practiced similarly to Islam; however, in the religion's age Judaisms believers did not recognize Mohammed's prophecy (the time of Jewish prophets ended 1000 years before Mohammad received his visit from the archangel Gabriel). Mohammed and his followers would conquer non-Islamic areas and levy taxes that supported conversion. The politics of the religion also supported religious freedom to a specific degree because Christians and Jews traveling to their respective holy lands were welcome to pay taxes for trade, travel, and stay in Islamic towns.

The religion would then spread via trade and exploration. As the religion began to take shape, a key component of the religion would promote economic stability to the region, its people, and the trade ports in their areas. One of Islam's five pillars is the Hajj. The Hajj is a pilgrimage to Mecca. When the religion was in its fledgling stages, it was a concern that the religion would usurp the economy and propel the citizens into poverty; however, the opposite resulted. For centuries the Hajj has promoted vast wealth to businesses with merchandise themed around the pilgrimage. The sacred journey would prove to be an extremely lucrative endeavor that helped religion and its politics spread throughout the world.

Christianity, another monotheistic religion, whose instituter, Jesus of Nazareth, a Jewish-born carpenter, lived a perfect life that would set the example for how his followers should live to achieve eternal life with life's creator and with him. Upon Christ's death and resurrection, the spread of Christianity would result in two kingdoms of vast riches in present times. The Catholic Church and the Orthodox Church would evolve from the Byzantine Empire and the Holy Roman Empire.

Similar to Islam, the spread of Christianity led to the creation of empires with great global power, authority, and wealth. Christianity would shape the world in so many ways that still have an impact felt 2000 years later.

Catholicism of the 14th century mandated the purchase, sale, and trade of African people as slaves to be used as the agricultural tools of colonization. Since the native people of the newly usurped colonies were dying from exposure to Christian settlers, the Pope, as a holy man and ruler, approved of the use of African slaves as labor hands instead of the explored land's native people. Africans had had centuries of experience intermingling with Europeans for trade as well as an adequate understanding of diverse tropical topography and engineering. Europeans would not have survived the "New World" without African ingenuity.

African slaves would lose their *African* -ness within 3 generations. By the time the first set of African slaves were bred, born, sold, and separated, the connection they shared with their motherland was gone. This would give rise to several centuries of Protestantism that would shape American history and find its practices to be manipulated by the issues of American slavery. [8]

Quakers, Methodists, and (Ana)Baptists are a few of the religious sects that grew from the seeds of American slavery. Quakers, Christian believers in the "primitive Christianity" are people who follow Jesus's teachings of nonviolent, simple living as well as taking up God's concern for the marginalized, and providing immediate and equal access to God's Spirit (as stated by the Quaker's organizational website). This form of Christianity was very different from the Christianity being practiced in Europe at that time.

It's important to understand European Christianity because it is intricately interwoven with government economics. In early Christianity, peasants (farmers) paid tribute for their land and belongings to the church and to the state. The "Church" was the wealthiest entity in the land and the State ruled the land. The Pope and the Monarchy worked closely with one another in determining the matters of the state. The Portuguese, Frank, Germanic, English, Scottish, Irish, Spanish, and Roman people would fight amongst themselves for land and authority as seen fit by God. They believed themselves to be led on Crusades for decades around the world and sought to grasp hold of resources under various rouses related to their interconnectedness with God.

---

8   Green, Toby. A Fistful of Shells: West Africa From the Rise of The Slave Trade to the Age of Revolution. Allen Lane / Penguin History, 2019.

When King Henry split from the Catholic Church to found the Church of England, the Anglicans would secure themselves a Christian lineage that granted England a plethora of riches that increased the country's monetary supply while supporting Parliament and the English monarchy in the 21st century. The English would colonize America, and their belief system would shape America by revolution, industry, policy, and allegiance.

When the Quakers arrived in America they brought with them an acumen for business and politics. Most Quakers settled in present-day Pennsylvania and New York. They were harsh abolitionists who supported the Underground Railroad, a secret network that helped free enslaved Americans from the plantations of the south. William Penn, a founding American Quaker, promoted tolerance and religious freedom. He was tolerant of native populations in America.

The Quakers challenged the beliefs of American (Ana) Baptists and Methodists. All of them shared the belief in Jesus, his movement, the Bible, and the sanctity of Christianity set forth by Paul. But, they all took differing stances on the economics of American Slavery.

Some American Baptists evolved from the Anabaptists of Europe. The Anabaptists believed in following the Bible and delaying baptism from that of infancy to a choice made when called. When Constantine met to unite Europe around Catholicism (universality). The Baptists disagreed with the members of the Council called by Emperor Constantine identifying them as heretics. These heretics faced constant persecution under Jewish rule, Roman rule, and the rule of Roman Catholicism. In the 16th and 17th centuries, the Anabaptists migrated to America.

During Reconstruction (7–10-year period after the Civil War), American Baptist, Methodists, and other Christian denominations established schools and businesses around education for America's newest taxpayer—the Negro. It was during this time that White apologists' strategy miseducated blacks into being docile subordinates fixated on being acknowledged as an equal human being by the American governing body (wealthy *white* elites).

African Methodist Episcopal Churches and the first established black church, First African Baptist would become railway stops on the Underground Railroad. Church members, administrators, and supporters helped the plantations enslaved blacks navigate north to freedom. The church would also influence black America's worship and religious practices today. Though not as influential in the 21st century as they were in the 1960s during America's Civil Rights movements, Black American clergy is often very respected.

The level at which the newly immigrated Americans approved of slavery was dependent on economic ability. Their religious affiliation was viewed in the number of working slaves and their treatment. Depending on the socioeconomic status of the believer, American slavery would ultimately be lucrative enough to finance and facilitate white supremacy. It also yielded the proliferation of fundamental and radical anti-integration social groups (EX: Ku Klux Klan and The Westboro Baptist Church).

Supremacy in its earliest understanding comes from King Henry VIII of England separating from the Catholic Church. Long story short: Henry wanted a divorce to try and have a male heir and the Pope of the time denied it. Henry enacted the Act of Supremacy 1534, saying that The King of England was also the overseer of the kingdom's religion and economy.

In 1763, France surrendered and gave America enough strength to revolt in 1765 and win its independence from Britain in 1787. America's independence won them an opportunity to develop their own government, economy, religious biases, and philosophy. Unfortunately, it was during this time that a black body was considered as human as a dairy cow. Ironically, the argument that blacks were property to be enslaved was best made in the plantation's chapel by church members with Bible verses.

America's success in war, land discovery, and global economy promoted a sense of pride in the white-skinned settlers capable of dropping their native culture and building a brand new one in America. It is common amongst white America to have ancestry who changed their surnames upon arriving in America. Upon the founding of the nation of America, the Supreme Court enacted a Supremacy ruling of its own.

Instead of a King holding all power over church and state, The Federal Government of America took power over resources and interpretation of the law. Article 6 of the Constitution of the United States of America says federal law and regulation supersedes state laws and regulations. Thankfully, the US has an army, navy, and law enforcement agency that has ensured blacks know just how to stay in line.

An important truth to come out of supremacy in both political forms across history is in the translation, printing, and distribution of the Christian faith's material. Multiple sects of Christianity have enabled the translation and dissemination of materials that citizens speaking the native language of the country use to shape their lives and familial beliefs and traditions. In England, this means the world has the King James translation of the Bible. In America, we have a nation built on multiple translations of the same doctrine, *The Constitution*. These translations dictate the interpretation of the law and handpicked the semantics that represents the nation and its people.

CHAPTER 2

THE BLACK STORY

"People evolve a language in order to describe and thus control their circumstances, or in order not to be submerged by a reality that they cannot articulate. (And, if they cannot articulate it, they are submerged.)"

— James Baldwin 1979

ESSENTIALLY, BITCOIN IS universal computer code; a system of rules written in a particular programming language. A language that is also a peer-to-peer decentralized protocol for a monetary network and currency. Elementarily, Bitcoin can be considered electronic cash that allows online payments to be sent directly from one party to another without going through traditional financial institutions.

In the United States of America, American slavery's legacy has empowered financial institutions (the legacy system) to amass wealth that has propelled the nation into becoming a prosperous militarized, technological, and industrialized nation. All of which was done at the expense of the descendants of America's free labor class, Black Americans.

The 1911 secret meeting of European bankers and American politicians resulted in more than the Federalist Reserve Act of 1913. This meeting forever indebted the American people to the country's financiers (German, British, Dutch) whose legacy would fund the country's "industrialization". This meeting solidified a denial of upward mobility to descendants of America's free labor class. The exclusion of prominent Black bankers and/or politicians from the meeting left black Americans to forever be considered an American asset turned liability[9].

Stripped of their native languages, the great-great-grandmothers of Black American millennials were treated on average as livestock. Anti-miscegenation laws and slave codes ensured blacks did not read, write, or gain status equal to the Europeans who migrated over after the 1000 years of financial peril known as the Dark Ages.

In making it illegal to read, write, and speak for themselves, Blacks were stripped of basic comprehension and communication skills. Communally, Black American's did not understand the language that signed the Declaration of Independence or negotiated the surrender at Appomattox. A language that forever unified America's immigrated Europeans into strong, proud, and globally appreciated White Americans. Misinterpretation of such monumental documents and the policies it upheld resulted in generations of miseducation,

---

9   Green, Toby. A Fistful of Shells: West Africa From the Rise of The Slave Trade to the Age of Revolution. Allen Lane / Penguin History, 2019.

economic exclusion, and political underrepresentation of Black Americans.

White Americans would grow to be the pride of the West. White Americans became titans, pioneers, settlers, and extremely successful CEOs. They were granted access to intermarry with the global monarchs and other early US financiers. They would become central bankers, world rulers, and politically protected diplomats.

Most destructively, having white skin granted the poorest American citizen the status of permanent overseer to Blackness. Depending on the beliefs of the Church tithed to, American whites were granted religious power to terrorize black Americans while white political groups were granted permission to gather and destroy Black America's economy with physical violence. Without a language to speak, Black Americans were left with a list of valueless vocabulary words spoken when addressed.

Former Africans were denied the ability to speak for themselves. The engineering of the slave trade was fueled by separating Africans and intermingling black-skinned people with other skin folk of different regions, cultures, and languages. Music became the language of the stolen and an appreciation of the elite. Hymns a spiritual cry of African pain, resiliency, and struggle also empowered enslaved people to hope, aim, and achieve freedom.

Chants, melodies, and harmonies that were once identifiers of occasion to foreign villages became support systems and travel networks. Hymns or "negro" spirituals, intricately designed hand-sewn quilts, and lullabies became sources of metaphysical communication amongst the only people the law punished for reading. Consequently, the Black language was a fountain of wealth for white exploiters.

The earliest evidence of this can be found in America's "Show" business (the entertainment industry). Storytelling is one of civilization's greatest pastimes. Depending on the culture, the story can be valued differently. As Immigrants became Americans, the stories became essential. Early American life was hard, so stories were told to make light of the situation and put the listener at ease while making an attempt to explain a complex topic or spread propaganda. Americans began to appreciate comedy more after the American Civil War.

The American Civil War was fought to ensure The United States of America remained united. Economically, the USA was growing into a global phenom. A fledgling country with a strong military, navy, and unlimited agricultural resources thanks to the free labor, civil engineering, and farming techniques provided by former Africans. As European immigrants evolved into white Americans, former Africans were concurrently turned into enslaved Americans. As a result of the South's succession, the enslaved became Black Americans devoted to democracy.

Black Americans would be hated in the South because their freedom indicated a huge economic bubble burst. America's economy suffered after the Civil War. Poor whites, wealthy land-owning families, and politicians took major financial losses when their most valuable asset no longer provided free labor. Freed Blacks became heavily resented, especially by those the War took everything from.

The stable "north" began to urbanize. As blacks migrated to America's northern region, resentments felt in the South would grow to be throughout the union. Blacks gained literacy within 3 years of freedom which demonstrated capability for employment and ultimately displayed their potentiality for success when interacting with the free market. Within seven years, Black Americans were on the way to establishing themselves as a competitive force equal to that of their White American counterpart. All of this was done during a time of high racial tension and aggression against non-whites.

Thomas Rice created the character, Jim Crow, based on an encounter with a Black American. His mockery and rendition of a song sung by an unknown Black created a genre of entertainment that was popular in mainstream culture for generations, Minstrelsy. As the North's population grew, factory life became harder for White American men. Minstrel show attendance became a beloved pastime in the North.

Without the interconnectivity of the internet, White Americans often created confirmation biases of life beyond their travel ability. After the Civil War "Southern Living" was stereotyped heavily. Entertainers made lots of money performing charades of plantation life and the newly formed Black American class. Minstrelsy ultimately shaped the stereotypes of blackness, southern living, and race relations for generations of Americans.

Rice popularized covering himself in burnt cork make-up and singing songs as if he were a black performing fool. Kindly put, he acted as an American man with a limited elementary understanding of grammar and social graces. He later created the Sambos, Coons, and Dandies archetypes that are hurtful and offensive to black people today—characters that would become the minstrel show staples. These characters also created the filters White Americans used to interpret blackness.

The 1914 establishment of the Central Banking System presented an opportunity for American policymakers to allow black Americans to participate in the USA's "free market" and never control it or change it[10]. Black Americans post-slavery were gaining confidence in capability. Despite the physical acts of terrorism inflicted on Black American people, Black Americans worked together to build communities with strong economies. Blacks began to speak the American language but did not understand the dialect. Black Americans began to travel, experience life, and report to one another in an ignored language. An example of this is found in the American music industry.

In 1944 an international meeting of financiers took place in Bretton Woods, New Hampshire because the Western world did not have enough gold. By this point, America had grown into a world power with a strong diverse military. The complete destruction of the global economy after two

---

10   Griffin, G. Edward. "What Creature Is This?" The Creature from Jekyll Island: A Second Look at the Federal Reserve, American Media, Westlake Village, CA, 2010, pp. 3–153.

world wars and a market collapse provided financiers an opportunity to take the world off the gold standard and profit from violence. This change in the global economy deceived people all over the world into putting value in paper money printed by private banks.

By the late 1940s, black music created the music genre, American Country, while simultaneously amassing huge revenue for the music industry with its own competing genre, "Race Music". White singers, musicians, and composers took expressions of Black Rhythm, Blues, Soul, and Gospel and whitewashed them to soothe the ears of American's who controlled the market.

Prior to Bretton Woods, Black Americans began to report blackness to each other purposely through art. The Renaissance of Harlem is a perfect example of the innovation and struggle of Black Americans. Blacks of the Renaissance created poems, plays, novels, and musical compositions that told the truth of Blackness. A year after the Bretton Woods Conference, Poet Langston Hughes published, *I, Too*. A poem criticizing the irony of America ignoring its Blacks because they are embarrassed by them and their history. Hughes and other artists expressed black empowerment, accomplishment, exploration through travel, and self-awareness with their Renaissance work.

The American economy climbed during the 1950s. The US's foundational layer of free labor and Byzantine political tactics of treachery, deception, and betrayal gave rise to America's middle class. Black American baby boomers would grow into passionate activists of the civil rights '60's. Unfortunately, they would prove to be the most misguided, disillusioned, and dynamic generation of modern history. The presumed success of social integration would destroy the economic progression and stunt the development of a strong Black American market competitor established pre-baby boom.

Black Boomers developed coping mechanisms that would yield monumental strides in comprehending America's language. Boomers learned to speak the language that made white Americans comfortable politically. It also assisted with limiting the elevation of Black empowerment.

Black Boomers made America's history socially digestible and nationalism marketable to investors around the world. Black Boomers raised children to become law-abiding citizens shushed away from questions and conversations that interrupted the imagery of American peace. Unfortunately, the misunderstanding of Black Boomers would give birth to generations of angry, lost, and traumatized children.

Destruction of social integration and misguidance of Black Boomers can be witnessed in the emergence and acclaim of *Hip Hop* music. It is being argued that hip-hop music originated as a language of the oppressed.

Young sons of American poverty— *the pioneers of Hip Hop*—established culture on four pillars: deejaying, emceeing, graffiti writing, and break dancing. In 1971, primarily black, Afro-Caribbean, and poor Latino teens held parties in New York where hip hop was allowed to develop into an industry for American export. Today hip hop is a multi-billion-dollar industry where the language of black people was heard, ignored, and used against the very people it was created to represent.

After the fall of Rome in 435 AD, Byzantium (Rome of the East) and its capital city, Constantinople remained financially intact. Emperor Constantine, a newfound Christian took control of the Roman Empire a century prior and built Constantinople. He founded an urban Christian City that would grow into an economic powerhouse with a strong army.

As the military grew, the amount of trust amongst its generals began to weaken. The people of the Byzantine Empire were divided into sports teams of blue and green. This division made it difficult to work together for the good of the empire. The Byzantine general's trust problem was solved by Satoshi Nakamoto in 2009; however, until the 21st century, this problem plagued the world well after the fall of the Byzantine Empire.

Mischievously, as European monarchs "explored" their way out of the Dark ages to establish the West, they unwittingly established another Empire with the same problems as Byzantium. As long as European immigrants were able to migrate and dream, America would provide them with a home country. However, for Black Americans once they became free, America turned into a nightmare for those already dreaming. The laws that ensured Blacks were unequal would be re-written to control the Black population and manipulate their narrative with the intent of helping everyone have an American dream.

In 1920, Carter G. Woodson wrote about the dangers of this "dream" in his book, *The Miseducation of the Negro*. Woodson argued that the most destructive thing to happen to Black Americans post-slavery was leaving the family and essentially the black community to become a part of White American society. Woodson thought it best for Blacks to have ownership, then establish a legacy around it instead of seeking white approval or becoming a black society pursuing whiteness.

Unfortunately, the opposing dialogue of accepted blacks, Harvard educated Dr. W.E.B Dubois and Orator, Educator Booker T. Washington confused America into ignoring Dr. Woodson. Ignoring Dr. Woodson essentially allowed Black Americans to develop into a community of continuously opposing teams. The division would be used to empower black miseducation for generations.

The dangers Dr. Woodson discusses in his writings are mimicked by black artists and entertainers that create with the freedom of blackness and communicate with the language established around the black American experience. The beat of the Harlem Renaissance was quieted by the bombings of the Second World War. Unbeknownst to most Americans, the financiers of the West waged war on the world to gain control of global resources and manipulate global markets, all in the name of Democracy.

After the war was won, America would return to a great global power (democracy) of great wealth and growth. America would become a safe haven for immigrants and refugees. Propaganda produced in Hollywood by America's growing cinema and entertainment industry ensured the world's most persecuted people, the Jews (as well as others threatened by a dictatorial rule), that there would be a tremendous opportunity for them in America. This opportunity disabled Black Americans and other descendants of American slavery to ever be considered oppressed or persecuted peoples.

A great example of this is witnessed in the iconic legacy of American Folk artist Bob Dylan, influenced heavily by the 1950's language of Black chronicler and performer Little Richard as well as by white musicians like Elvis Presley whose exploitation of Black culture titled him the "king" of Rock and Roll. A Jewish child born in Minnesota, Bob Dylan was famous for his songs that questioned America's race relations. In his 1963 song, "Blowing in the Wind" Dylan questions how long until black Americans have the independence to be free. Dylan claims the answer is found blowing in the wind and therefore, unattainable.

As he continued to write protests songs and question the establishment throughout the decade, his fame overshadowed the change that would come to black America as Civil Rights leaders were assassinated for asking for economic equality for Black citizens. Boomer activism grew into political and corporate involvement throughout the Civil Rights Era.

Black Americans began to accept the social inclusion of integration, ignore the damage integration caused to the Black community, and pretend change had come. We experienced pseudo-change, a manipulation of common language to be used to communicate deceit via legislative policy.

Pseudo-change empowered Blacks to shed their blackness for white-collar respect and blue-collar luxuries. Blacks began to put on costumes and persuade white Americans of their exceptionality due to their ability to speak with the accent of those in power.

Hip hop emcee Ice Cube eloquently expresses the monster birthed by the protesting and activism of the 1960s, law enforcement terrorism. In his lyrical masterpieces of the 1980s, Ice Cube discusses the physical acts of aggression that Blacks throughout the country experienced at the hands of the untouchable police. A problem similar to the Byzantines, Black Americans could not trust or communicate with one another because Blacks who've chosen to wear the blue costume of the police are more treacherous than their white brethren.

The blue uniform of law enforcement made it difficult for black-skinned Americans to trust that the law would protect them. Thanks to the rebellious acts of hip hop's originators, Black chroniclers had a platform to express the turmoil caused by the "protections" of the 1960s. Artists like Public Enemy, Rakhim, and Ice T discussed the mistrust and disdain towards the judicial system and America's law enforcement agency.

The unjust 1991 beating of Rodney King by white police officers in California was video evidence of the terrorism black Americans experienced at the hands of the government and its law enforcing agents. Tupac Shakur would emerge as a chronicler of Black oppression, and the consequences poverty and economic exclusion had on black Americans. His work would stir a sense of rebellion in the Boomer-built suburbs of White America.

Coupled with the grunge scene coming out of the pacific northwest, teenage white Americans were growing frustrated with the obligatory path of the Boomers. Though the 1980s were a time of great employment and the establishment of the middle class because black and white boomers were college-educated and earning solid wages. Black boomers spoke the language of the power holders better than the language of their people and Carter G. Woodson's warning became a premonition for the lives and experiences of the Boomers' grandchildren.

As different accents of the King's English became universally understood as the language of America's elite; hip-hop became the language of the American criminal. In looking at the evolution of Tupac Shakur's artistry, it's clear that his criminal record grew alongside his fame. In his short lifetime, he was released from state custody more times than he released an album.

In the present-day US, hip-hop artists await indictment and sign multimillion-dollar recording contracts at the same time. Their credibility is determined by their criminality. This shift in understanding happened when Black artistry started influencing the behavior of white American youth. In the 1990s, white teens began to learn and speak the language of Black America, no longer needing a white interpreter to whitewash the black sound.

An awakening to black sensibilities frustrated America's political infrastructure to persecute black poverty and redefine it as rebellious acts of criminality. Now the language of the oppressed became an identifier of the criminal. The truth about drugs in black neighborhoods, crooked police officers, and government-facilitated "gang" violence would be ignored as the recording industry grew into a narrative controlling tyrant.

The recording industry would gain control and reshape black expression. When whites no longer needed black music to generate revenue for the white artist, executives began to influence black Americans into exploiting their own voices. Protest music and honest lyrical compilation once told undiscussed facts of black American oppression and terrorism shifted into advertisements that promoted the image of blackness white America is comfortable digesting, criminal.

Hip hop music of the late 1990s like Black culture throughout America's history, was divided. Artists such as Lauryn Hill, Yasin Bey, Outkast, Erykah Badu, Nas, and Common provided advice and perspective to blacks having an American experience, while Jay Z, Too Short, Snoop Dogg, and Lil Kim promoted industry idealism of gang banging hyper sexualized drug dealers, prostitutes, and pimps. As those who grew disenfranchised with the industry shifted the use of their platforms, those who encouraged white comforts became industry executives and culture dictators who evolved into black "leaders".

The mainstream music of Y2k was filled with angst and advertisements. Designer fashion brands, luxurious vehicles, and scantily clad women became the socialization vectors for how black Americans determined value. Exotic dancing replaced an ancestral art form that acted as a metaphysical language between deities and the ones they protected. This made room for the popular "Twerk" dance exported along with hip-hop culture.

> "The brutal truth is that the bulk of white people in America never had any interest in educating black people, except as this could serve white purposes. It is not the black child's language that is in question, it is not his language that is despised: It is his experience. A child cannot be taught by anyone who despises him, and a child cannot afford to be fooled."
>
> — James Baldwin 1979

CHAPTER 3
BLACK WOMAN'S ORATORY

I haven't lived long but it has been a good life.
Troubles come, people go
a revolving door of circumstance, hardship, and triumphs.
As a child, I'd ask my mother about this life.
She'd say, "take your time and live".

As a teen, my best friend got sick.
Disease spread from her broken heart to her GOD-fearing
    brain.
Alzheimer's,
the name the doctor kept usin'.
Every time I'd check on Grandma to see how she was doin'
she'd smile and reassure me
"just fine".

When I was to graduate high school,
Cancer would take residence
inside my mother's breast.
Surgery, chemotherapy, and radiation
all used to exorcise the demon

monopolizing her chest.
Five years later,
that cancer that "left",
spread to her lungs and forced out her last breath.

Freshman year of college,
brought with it its own stress.
Prematurely giving my first boyfriend,
my entire self
with hopes of loving him
in sickness and in health
3 years 8 months later,
the relationship met its death.

That boy that I loved
would go on to disrespect my body
and
shit on my heart.
Contributed to my breaking,
leaving me alone in my weakness
and our friendship destroyed.
We'd met in high school
and spoke to each other every day.
Him,
The quiet, mysterious type
long dark hair with dark eyes.
Me,
a bright-eyed jolly little fool.

I was the school welcome committee
addicted to teen romance novels.
Him, burnout "cool".
My very first love,
with him, I planned my future
in him, I put my trust.
I tried and failed to make him stay
because I thought I could make him
change.
A long-winded drama with a tragic ending
turned out to be exactly
what I needed.
An important lesson was learned.

Life was a circus
when lusting for that boyfriend.
We both made clowns of ourselves.
Dancing on a tightrope,
juggling the anticipation
awaiting a physical reaction
anxiety over the danger,
— consequence of the characters losing control.
Loving him was difficult.
A mirror reflecting the environment at home.
Discomfort and confusion,
all he'd ever known.
Since we have stopped dating
I am sure he has grown.

From the bitter boy
who sent missiles to my reputation
character and name.
He's experienced highs and unfathomable lows
so
I continually pray for his soul and hope
Jesus will be the one
he comes to love and know.
Thankfully,
this has all been left in the past.
If anyone were to ask,
I am living my life,
taking my time,
doing just fine.

And I bought some Bitcoin.

I THOUGHT I HAD a sincere understanding of death when my Momma died. Lying on the driveway, with the sun beaming on my face and my heart pounding strongly against the cold pavement, it suddenly dawned on me that she was leaving. I realized at that moment there was no turning back.

I spent the last year grieving the overdose of my live-in ex and reassuring my mom that I would "stick to the plan": graduate, get a job, and then enroll at a med school. You know, the too-familiar plan, which parents of so-called, "advanced/

high achieving" students have to follow. Six months after getting my diploma, studying for MCAT turned into missing a GRE so I could take my Momma the comforts needed for long hospital stays.

Her pneumonia treatment became chemotherapy. Before I understood what was happening, the doctor's signs of improvement transitioned into my Momma struggling on a ventilator to say, "The nurses won't let me die."

On March 13, 2018, my mom was ready to go. After talking to her doctors, I realized there was absolutely no way to find a compromise. She would die if they took the tube out.

My grandmother passed the crown of Matriarch to my mom. Momma hosted, organized, and assisted every family gathering. Somehow, in all her organizing, she was never able to get a consensus on the dessert menu.

Whatever she wanted to make, nobody wanted to eat, so we compromised — a decision that left us with far too many leftovers. Unfortunately, sweet potato pie or banana pudding is irrelevant when the debate is about living attached to a ventilator.

Momma and I had a conversation some time before that very moment. I had to put myself aside, be still, and find silence when she boldly apologized for the pain her absence would cause me. She said, "I should've listened to you and taken better care of myself. You were right; I was wrong." Having had that conversation, I signed the papers and started the process of taking her off the ventilator.

For some reason, I was expecting the process to be scary. I found myself comforted with every IV change and detachment, knowing my Momma was getting what she wanted. Ultimately, I was being obedient and that always made her happy.

In the weeks, months, and years immediately after her passing, I was forced to remember her lessons and continue building upon my foundation; a task she trained me for. Unfortunately, in my preparedness, I was disappointed, humbled, and forever changed as our loved ones figured out how to live without the family keystone.

Social media discourse and constant reminders of "unity" from the people paying the celebrities caused me to dislike aspects of my core identity and feel lost. It was March 13, 2020, and Breonna Taylor was killed on the 2nd anniversary of my mother's passing. All I could do is hum, *Jesus loves me*.

It's silly, but that's what my mom would sing to me as I anxiously walked to my 8 AM Biology Exams. I remember laughing at her as I opened the doors of the Clendenin building at KSU. She was always "pulling into the school," hurrying me off the phone and simultaneously reminding me to sing it to myself if I "got flustered." It worked up until the semester my now late boyfriend bought bitcoin for dabs.

I didn't sleep well the night Breonna Taylor was murdered. I was too busy realizing that she could have been me, especially considering that we were the same age. Being a young lady in love—blissfully ignorant of life outside the safe space your partner provides—was no longer a shield of protection from gross mischaracterization, exploitation, or unjustified criminality.

Three years prior, I learned to understand the importance of accountability after the overdose of my ex-boyfriend. His ability to hide his addiction, his family's avoidance of the problem, and the misjudgment of my character all revealed the importance of taking accountability and living honestly.

Come June 2020, Rayshard Brooks, an unarmed black man, was murdered after an "incident" at a Wendy's. I can remember being at school laughing with childhood friends as they joked about their "drunk" somebody getting too excited to celebrate and falling asleep in the drive-thru. As the Wendy's, where he was killed burned, I started having questions.

Traumatic images were everywhere. Fortunately, during my mom's time with chemotherapy, I found value in eating fresh fruits and raw vegetables. Upon her passing, I chose to allow my diet to act as my body's medicine and decided to stop eating processed and fried foods. As the numbers rose, I remember feeling confused that nutrition was not being discussed in the "Covid-19" arguments.

I started to notice huge industries associated with internalized trauma were making large profits while my local bar closed down for good. I could not miss the six degrees of Big Pharma, Big Sugar, Big Tech, and the banks as they profited off people like my momma: American, honest, hardworking, and stressed.

My mom was a black, unwed, single mother. She left me to take care of the bulk of her arrangements, debts, and assets at

23. When she left, I was forced to stop living based on feelings and emotions. It was time to grow up.

I had to start following paper trails. I read and listened more in order to comprehend life's nuance. If I made a bad financial decision, there was nobody to bail me out. I became accountable for every dollar I spent.

Then, I started to learn about debt. I was taught to avoid debt by only paying for what I could afford, and if ever I had to borrow, I was taught to pay the bill on time and as quickly as possible. All in all, I learned debt should always be avoided.

In having that basic understanding of debt, I grew immensely distrustful of the social justice protesting that sprang up across America. Virtue signaling organizations sprang up like grass in May, all in hopes of defending their pursuits of justice and gaining financial support from the public.

Content creators misrepresented themselves as leaders, activists, and social justice warriors for donated funds, loans, and poorly understood stimulus checks. Only for the 2020 election to reveal these characters to be self-serving clout chasing money grabbers. Their balance sheets held profits as the people who donated to them continued to wait for unemployment.

The "fight for: justice, equality, and reparations" was inundated with trivial political maneuvers such as a national holiday announcement and some political appointments; maneuvers that all share the common historical theme of solution avoidance, especially when it comes to Black

Americans. Political decrees that make the atmosphere "feel" like change even though the perceived growth is minuscule compared to the devastation caused by a generational mischaracterization of the black man.

The truth is there is not enough money, land, or resources to adequately repay Black Americans for the contribution of their ancestors. For lack of better understanding, there is not enough money to ensure the Black lives that people march for actually matter. The window of repayment ran out with the signing of the Federal Reserve Act by Woodrow Wilson in 1913.

Protests, demonstrations, and other "acts of rebellion" are nothing more than untapped sources of revenue for government agencies. The banks and their subsidiaries make money from violence and its derivative, trauma. The more I learned about debt, the more I learned about the banks and the violence the central bank supports.

A couple of months after my mother passed, I felt reassured in my decision to cremate her as opposed to the traditional ceremony that my family preferred. The plan was to bury her until I heard the price. I told her my decision, and she nodded with acceptance. We compromised.

The burial insurance policy was the exact amount of a burial, almost 20x the cost of cremation. It was the largest check I had ever seen. It was my money, and the company that sent the check was definitely good for it, yet it took 14 days for the bank to process my deposit.

I started having questions about account fees, interest rates, and taxes. Trying to find the answers led to more questions. I started to feel like I would end up like my mother, working my entire life just to pay bills and die.

I started having suicidal ideations when I went back to work 2.5 weeks after my mom passed. As a part-time (PT) hire working full-time, I was forced to resign from my cherished guest relations job at a premier engineering company because I was uninsured and PT positions did not offer disability benefits.

In corporate America, mental health is only a disability for the insured. After losing my job and venting my financial frustrations to a friend, he told me about Bitcoin.

Up until then, I understood Bitcoin as the thing that helped my late ex-boyfriend purchase what I thought were THC concentrates. I blamed Bitcoin for enabling his opioid disease to spread throughout his life like a lethal contagion. I was wrong. Bitcoin is a financial tool that empowers freedom. With every choice, there is a consequence. In the case of my ex, the repercussion of the way he chose to exercise his freedom was fatal.

Bitcoin, a decentralized, peer-to-peer currency network answers many of the questions I was having about my finances. In learning about Bitcoin, I learned about the government and its relationship with the banks. I also learned real "reparations" would decimate our dollars' spending power.

The government is made of teams that claim to represent the common masses. These teams are forced to rival one another in an attempt to accomplish common goals aimed at making life profitable for the country's sponsors. The sponsors are all tied to financiers of any given government's independent inception.

In 21st century America, the ties to these sponsors are as strong as family bonds. They are international, multi-generational, and multi-disciplinary. Their wealth is a common thread amongst them all as the acquisition of said wealth is seldom overlooked.

Much has to do with the exploitation of people via religion, natural resources, and time theft. Time and American history reveal their ancestors' manipulation of the global "free" market has a disastrous fate. Fortunately, Bitcoin offers a solution to that problem as well.

On my 10th birthday, a friend introduced the "what would you do" game at the party. I was excited to play it with my mom to know what she would do with a billion dollars. I don't think I'll ever forget how silent it was when she responded, "I'll never have it."

Dissatisfied with her answer, I ignored it to tell her exactly what I would do with it. Again, she was right. She would never see it and the way the financial system was designed, she wasn't supposed to.

Bitcoin is a financial tool that restores hope, especially to those who feel hopeless around the world. In dealing with the finances after my mom's passing, I started to become nauseated with the truth surrounding the circumstances of her death. Simply put, she had to die.

Financially, the cost of her life would have devastated mine. Cancer treatment, diabetes treatment, heart disease treatment, and the mortgage would have been more than I could handle alone. Through her death, I learned the meaning of sacrifice with that revelation I became fixated on ensuring her legacy was protected. Bitcoin was a tool that offered a solution.

Bitcoin is an asset that protects the most expensive asset known to man, time. My mom was relatively young in her passing; she was given 51 years, 29 of which she worked weekends, late evenings, and early mornings.

My mother took her job seriously and more importantly; she served Black Children like it were her duty. In her passing, all of her debtors called for collection. Probate courts took a portion for themselves in settling housing disputes and offering condolence.

Bitcoin is deflationary. In purchasing small amounts of Bitcoin (SATS), every dollar exchanged for my time will be worth more in the future. Another example of a deflationary tool is technology. Technological innovation makes life easier and capable of becoming more efficient over time.

Six months after dealing with my mom's passing, I was becoming more frustrated with my interactions with the bank. I kept running into situations where I was completely at the bank's mercy for money that belonged to me.

My mother sacrificed her time to work so I would be able to live without her, and the banks deserved some. Why? It's designed that way. Fractional reserve banking means the money I deposited into my "account" is nothing more than a loan that I'm involuntarily making to the bank in exchange for whatever they choose to give me (interests rate), after fees.

Bitcoin is the only currency that offers protection against the selfish monopolistic establishment of the current financial institution. Bitcoin offers the holder of satoshi the ability to store/keep/handle their money themselves. The wallet that they hold the passkeys to is theirs to manipulate.

Bitcoin was introduced to the world in 2009. A sacrifice of Satoshi Nakamoto as a consequence of the narcissism and crony capitalism associated with the 2008 global housing fumble. A fixed time-released supply offered a time-stamped solution for the double-spend problem, counterfeiting.

Bitcoin allows the unbanked to have safe access to currency across the entire world. Over time, Bitcoin evolved into a layered system spread across a global network of nodes that utilize cheap, untapped energy from natural resources to ensure the impenetrable system continues to run. The network is currently 12 years old and the sixth-largest currency in the world (and rising).

This is a consequence of scarcity. Bitcoin is scarce—the USD is the total opposite—a reason being it is printed at the whim of the Federal Reserve Bank. Bitcoin is mined via computer science, code. The code ensures a time-release of the 21 Million Bitcoin until they all have been mined in 2140. Bitcoin is such an honest currency that June 2021 brought about a monumental geopolitical validation of Bitcoin's capabilities when El Salvador became the first country in the world to enact bitcoin as legal tender.

An extremely poor nation devastated by poverty from oligarchic destruction similar to that experienced by Black America is front-running what some are calling "the greatest wealth transfer in financial history". Several other countries devastated by poverty and the volatility surrounding the USD are looking into Bitcoin to solve their financial problems.

I began to question the way I wore my blackness. My momma raised me to love it. She made it clear in telling me she chose to have me. That meant my daddy being African was deliberate. In choosing to love every aspect of myself during a time when it has never been harder; I spent the global lockdown understanding who I am.

I spent more time reading about blackness than I did scrolling, defending, and blocking folks about it. I learned about the purposefully omitted history of Ancient Africans, the contribution of early African servants turned American citizens whose architecture enabled Europeans to settle in the tropical-like climate of Virginia. I learned of the cat and mouse game that lawmakers played with African settlers to ensure them no rights worth honoring by their white counterparts.

Analogous to a single parent of fraternal twins, the twin most resembling the prime custodian is spoiled with excess, while the other is neglected or lovingly dismissed. Modern-day Black America is a descendant of an excruciatingly large loss of wealth. What some consider a devastating blow to the Confederacy can be argued to have been a blow to the nation.

Whereas white immigrants had financial incentives to start colonies, banks, military ports, and universities within the boundaries of an already civilized nation. Enslaved Africans were stripped of their identities and their new status of "negro" became the economy's greatest asset. Federal emancipation turned these assets into market manipulating liabilities.

In the seven years after the Civil War, Black Americans capabilities were infinite. Blacks had a high literacy rate. There was also an emergence in black banks, schools, farms, and businesses. Had the market remained free, there is no telling the ingenuity to have shaped the world.

Unfortunately, fear of retribution for the crimes of slavery led to a manipulation of the market that divided the nation in more ways than one; all the while Ponzi-ing a debt too big to repay at the expense of the financier's newfound labor class, Middle America.

As a millennial, a Black American woman, and a lover of history, I choose to take accountability for my life and pick differently. Bitcoin is my choice. It is my option out of hopelessness. Bitcoin reinforced the confidence in my blackness I was taught to love openly as a child.

Bitcoin is the compromise of Booker T Washington and W.E.B Dubois. Bitcoin enables us all to have our own while simultaneously working and contributing to society in ways that benefit everybody. Bitcoin restores competition, which fosters innovation and allows inhabitants of the planet to heal themselves of generational trauma.

I have absolutely no idea what the future holds. I just know that following tradition without knowing the origin can be expensive to a person's identity. The traditional money network I am accustomed to is also very expensive. It cost my mother her life.

Bitcoin and the accompanying Lighting Network are being developed by some of the most dedicated and profoundly apt human beings on the planet. They do this all with similar goals. Protection and implementation of a decentralized open-source network that enables individuals to have sovereignty over their time via their wealth.

Although Bitcoin was around when my mom was alive, I was too busy "being young" to understand it. At that point in my life, I was interested in "college life", making A's, and boosting my GPA. The most profound questions I explored were why sororities weren't interested and why I even cared.

The other end of immaturity's double-edged sword, youth, taught me lessons I'm blessed to have not lost my life learning. There have been so many like my ex-boyfriend, Breonna Taylor, and even Ross Ulbricht who have lost their lives in their youth. I was blessed to make it down my momma's proverbial "fool's hill."

After high school in 2012, my mom suggested I start a business, look into the stock market, or take up a "cyber" field instead of going the traditional debt-fueled Biology route to medical school. I didn't agree. I was enjoying my climb up "fool's hill," collecting snap views and insta-likes while tapping the bottom of unopened liquor bottles.

In the four years since my mother died, I have lost my job, severed familial ties, matured to wine drinking, and managed to preserve my mother's legacy with Bitcoin. In a sense, I deviated from the original plan but in doing so, I managed to uncover entrepreneurial passions she begged me to explore.

The death of my ex taught me gumption. It encouraged me to take accountability and listen with my eyes to observe with my ears. It led me to be more prepared for losing my mother. My mother encouraged me to be a free thinker; she insisted I avoid labels and cliques, she taught me the importance of character and integrity, so thinking of her at peace brings me immense joy and thankfully, Bitcoin offers a moral currency option that enables me to continue to celebrate her. As I continue to live life according to her teachings, I find myself full of gratitude. I am grateful for Bitcoin and the opportunity it affords my future. More importantly, I am grateful for the foundation my mother laid.

I didn't learn about Bitcoin as money until my mother had been in heaven a year by earth's standards. In learning about Bitcoin, I realized my A's and B's in economics meant absolutely nothing. I learned that I was never taught about money. I was taught how to be an upstanding contributing member to a society brown-skinned people have been indebted to since the system's conception. It's imperative for Black America to get on board with Bitcoin. I believe in GOD, I believe in Jesus, I believe in the holy spirit, and I believe in Bitcoin.

Black Americans have been terrorized into believing, trusting, and ignoring the things that are everything but good for them. Negotiations with the government resulted in "equality" for every disenfranchised group black people happened to fall into but didn't quite make it up. This has damaged us as a people to the extent of hopelessness. At this point, we have dwindled ourselves down to a block vote adding flavor to stale politics.

Bitcoin is a global currency. A type of money that reinforces sovereignty, allowing the earner to possess and manage his wealth. A system completely opposite of the current money (fiat) system that we have grown up valuing and appreciating.

CHAPTER 4

BITCOIN: STORY OF THE FUTURE

"Ahsh,

I don't want you smokin' my money away."

— a final conversation

between mother and daughter

THERE WAS SO much weight packed into that short conversation. Love, grief, fear, and disappointment each ten pounds of added pressure to the concept of rationalizing a losing battle with cancer. The least heavy force but equally important necessity of being smart with a harvest the planter would never be able to taste or enjoy.

Upon her transition, there was a grave necessity to do the right thing in every aspect of life post-mom. Even though I was to trust absolutely no one; tell absolutely no one what was left behind. The only thing I could do was pray and meditate. I couldn't eat or dance.

In my quietest moments, the spirit would speak to me with memories. I would remember conversations, interactions, have crystal clear images. Instead of fear, pity, or nostalgia, I felt invigorated and overjoyed. Trusting in that and believing in Jesus, I found that I knew exactly what to do.

1. Take care of *everything* with an expiration date.
2. *Prioritize.* Handle what needs to get handled, pray.
3. Make decisions create a plan.
4. Pray.
5. Execute the plan and organize follow-up.
6. Follow up... follow through.

Then I met a man. A very strong-willed man that needed me just as much as I needed him. Neither of us knew we were praying for the other.

This man, a bitcoin pleb, would challenge me in every way that made me stronger. The most important—financially. In loving a man and telling him absolutely nothing about my finances, he increased my net worth by introducing me to Satoshi Nakamoto.

Satoshi Nakamoto, the anonymous entity that developed and implemented Bitcoin. An honest money system that incentivizes humanity's capacity for good. A money system that genuinely helps those who've been oppressed by the implementation of the historic monetary system that have made Europeans and their descendants egregiously rich.

That was 2018. I was tired of them killing black people for all media to dissect in 2016 with the slaying of Philando Castille. In 2016, I fought with all my strength for Gary Johnson to have the opportunity to debate. I could not believe how many American adults, people that I grew up respecting, were okay with adults on a national (with the internet, global) stage acting in a way that would have caused me to get a punishment.

It is only name calling and unfortunate entertainment when rich, white, blondes from New York do it. It was ghetto and ineffective communication when I did it. Either way, Gary did not debate. I did not vote.

Then Trump won, and America pretended to be shocked. Blacks got doubled down on; every stereotype and euro-narrative created was perpetuated in the media. Reinforcing and reminding us just how powerless we were. Some of us started waking up and trying to tell others unfortunately, Bodak Yellow dropped.

It's November 2018, and this white boy and his roommates will not shut up about Bitcoin. One roommate, short with a name of aspirational heights and the other an immigrant from Brazil.

February 2020, America is in the midst of a nationwide shutdown, and I have the realization that black America is an endangered nation. If we are not deliberate, we could be as extinct as the Natives. Come March, George Floyd is murdered and the air smells like Gomorrah as North Central California becomes Sodom, engulfed in flames.

Perilousness, loneliness, and bold courage permeate through my being as friendships come to an end and realizations are made that I need to better educate myself on the world and being African American. Then, I read Isaiah Jackson's *Bitcoin and Black America*.

It's simple: Black Americans have been miseducated. Bitcoin offers correction and authority in a country that was designed, engineered, and built by our forefathers. It is on the back of slaves that America is built therefore with Bitcoin and an education system focusing on re-education and redefinition of blackness; Black America can re-establish itself as a nation within a nation.

Bitcoin and its principles yield black Americans an opportunity to reclaim what was taken from our forefathers by acquiring what was stolen. Bitcoin offers ultimate protest. It allows us to become the revolutionaries that Fred Hampton died convincing us to be.

"Bitcoin is a lifeboat."
— Jeff Booth; Podcast with Raoul Pal 9/24/2020

For as long as I can remember, money was a topic somebody I loved needed, wanted, lost, won, or found. Checks were always getting cashed and every other Friday was payday. I genuinely had no idea what money was; I just knew my momma felt like she could never be a millionaire. I found comfort in knowing Jesus was born to the least of the world; Jesus was born into poverty, too.

Black Americans have been tricked into believing rich "whiteness" was man's ultimate desire. The black American celebrity reinforced that psychology by brandishing expensive products afforded to them by the supporters that can't afford it themselves. It's a vicious cycle. A cycle implanted within a people to keep them disillusioned into an underclass status to prop up an entire country's economy.

Black Americans born in the past 30 years have been born into a system where they are the least in their homeland. Black Americans have been born into belief systems that only make sense when disillusioned about the truth. Marching and exercising rights to gather, protest, and demand equality only make sense when the belief is black America has "overcome" and continues to "overcome". Overcome what? Slavery? What kind of slavery?

"The last shall be first and the first shall be last"
— Jesus Christ, Matthew 20:16

Bitcoin rectifies wrongs against Black Americans that the American government is too far down the sewage hole to correct. It is absolutely asinine to think Black Americans will ever receive adequate reparations for the atrocities that have been happening against us since the Klan ended reconstruction.

Bitcoin offers black American families opportunity to continue to work every day and not feel enslaved by the monotony of "trying to make it". It allows even the lowliest worker to feel as though their time working is valuable. Especially when it's something they love to do and can teach their children.

Instead of the hardworking single mother feeling as though she will never have wealth believing she has no options because the supplies she needs to live increase in price year after year; she can now transfer enough of that money into a system that will help her gain stability in more ways than one. Bitcoin gives America's most disenfranchised group a dignity that is genuinely inherent to natural beings.

Bitcoin changes the dynamic of the home so much so that it can change the ecosystem of the housing projects. Bitcoin makes the "hood" safe how the United States Dollar (USD) made it dangerous. The fiat system, money, how we understand it made black lives, especially Black men, a sequence of numbers. Whether numbers of incarceration or numbers on a death certificate—all of which make up FBI statistics—the USD has ruled everything around black men since before the US government flooded the hoods with guns and drugs.

Bitcoin is personal and private. It's so valuable you don't want to spend it or brag to others about how much you have. That very quality of this currency protects people forced to live on-top of one another in urban developments.

Bitcoin makes all the atrocities of the past just that, atrocities of the past. When Black Americans fully adopt and implement Bitcoin as a security measure against a government that has proven time and time again to not care about our safety/protection, then all the pain of our ancestors will live on, but when the system falls, we rise.

BITCOIN Q & A

WHY DO I NEED BITCOIN?

The government cannot afford to return any promises made to black Americans for reparation. It is far more beneficial for an individual of any capacity to hold their own wealth, dictate their prices without chargebacks, and verify that the exchange in question is fair and valid. Multiple streams of income are far easier with Bitcoin than the current financial system. Never before in history have average and impoverished people been given the ability to hold an unconfiscatable money. This money is even protected from violent overtaking.

I CAN'T AFFORD BITCOIN. CAN I BUY ANOTHER CHEAPER COIN?

You can do whatever you want. You do not need anyone to do anything for you. You have the choice to be yourself and educate yourself.

The "cheaper coins" however do not solve the same problem bitcoin does. They are not the same. Buying those coins present you with the risk of losing your entire investment. Exchanges that sell them are online casinos.

YOU CAN DEFINITELY AFFORD TO BUY BITCOIN.

Bitcoin wasn't designed for every individual to have an entire coin, but it was designed to sustain the world as a global reserve currency.

1 Bitcoin is comprised of 100 million sats and therefore it can be purchased in pieces. No matter the quantity of sats, the longer you hold them, the more value you have.

IF THE BANKS, THE GOVERNMENT, A COMPANY, AND/OR A MASTER SERVER DO NOT RUN BITCOIN AND DO NOT DICTATE THE PRICE. WHAT MAKES BITCOIN SO VOLATILE? WHY IS IT ALWAYS GOING UP AND DOWN?

There is volatility in absolutely every aspect of life. The Law of Entropy enlightens the world that the universe tends towards disorder.

The price of Bitcoin is dependent on the spending patterns of the Bitcoin network's transactors. Therefore, the price goes down when people sell their sats and the price goes up when people buy sats and when they take the sats off of exchanges and put them into cold storage.

Bitcoin is more about the future than it is about the present. People who buy Bitcoin are buying it knowing that it will be worth more in the future than it is today.

WHAT MAKES BITCOIN DIFFERENT FROM THE MONEY WE ALREADY HAVE?

The money that we have today is corrupt. The USD holds the status of Global Reserve Currency, which means many countries in the world base the value of their country's wealth on the value of the United States' Dollar. The United States' Dollar was once extremely valuable however, with every stimulus check, infrastructure bill, and promise of protection, the USD started to lose its value. The money is corrupt in that it has created the illusion that it is so valuable it's worth dying for. That is simply not true. The dollar is only as valuable as the people who have faith in it.

Bitcoin is different because of its protocol. Bitcoin is designed to be scarce. There are 21 million bitcoin and will only ever be 21 Million Bitcoin. There can be less (loss of keys), but there will never be more. Bitcoin is on a time release schedule with a mining reward that is reduced by 1/2 every 4 years. In 2140, there will no longer be new bitcoin being added to the supply.

WHERE DO I BUY BITCOIN?

Bitcoin can be purchased from a plethora of avenues. Online casinos that sell alt-coins typically sell bitcoin. However, it is not recommended that you purchase Bitcoin from those places. It is best that Bitcoin is purchased from a reputable bitcoin only company like Strike and SwanBitcoin. You can also buy Bitcoin peer to peer from a person who holds bitcoin and is willing to sell them to you in person. When purchasing bitcoin, the most important thing is knowing that your bitcoin can be taken off the exchange and held offline in cold storage. The only way a Bitcoin can be held is if the key to the wallet is in the possession of the bitcoin purchaser.

I STORE MY MONEY IN THE BANK. HOW WOULD I STORE MY BITCOIN?

Storing money in the bank is something that we have been conditioned to believe is good because we, as people who work for the money, aren't smart enough to hold onto it. It was then believed that banks holding money was a sign of status and helped people with money make money off their money via interests. Ultimately, by allowing banks to hold our money, we are giving them the ability to spend it and do with it as they please. If it's lost then there is more opportunity to print the money as insurance to the account holder.

Bitcoin can be stored in a variety of ways. The first is considered hot storage. Being a hot wallet means a third party holds the keys to the sats in the wallet. Muun Wallet is a good example and shitty online casinos are bad examples of hot storage. Muun Wallet is my favorite reputable hot storage company because it makes Bitcoin and lightning transactions incredibly streamline. It also has an incredible user interface for someone who is bored with technology. Remember, this is not the most secure way of storing Bitcoin but it is efficient.

Cold storage is the most secure form of storage. Cold storage means the keys are held by the bitcoin purchaser and taken offline. There are various forms of cold storage that deserve to be researched and chosen as a means of storing and protecting Bitcoin. I suggest Casa in tandem with ColdCard by coinkite.

IF BITCOIN ISN'T A BUSINESS; WHY ARE THERE FEES WHEN I BUY AND TRANSACT IN SATS?

Bitcoin is comprised of 3 parts that are all equally important to maintaining its protocol.

1. **Holders (hodlers) =** Hodlers are simply people who buy and hold bitcoin. They are the ones who spend and save sats daily. They cause the volatility in the market. Hodlers' demand influences price.

2. **Nodes =** Nodes validate and verify the transactions being made as they are loaded onto the blockchain. They offer the network a layer of protection that secures the network from bad actors in that they don't allow false transactions. There are different types of nodes and anyone can build and run their own.

3. **Miners =** Miners solve the shah 256 algorithm that increases the supply of sats in the market; they also keep the time schedule. As payment for the hard work that it takes these energy converting computers to open the next block, they receive block rewards for transactions. Lightning is a layer that has been added on top of Bitcoin's network that makes fees faster and cheaper.

HOW DOES BITCOIN WORK? WHAT HAPPENS IF THE POWER GOES OUT?

Bitcoin is energy. Therefore it can be powered with any form of energy. If the power goes out, it can be powered by water, wind, solar, and thermoelectrical energy.

Even if there were no internet Bitcoin could be mined by hand and paper wallets traded peer to peer.

BITCOIN HAS BEEN AROUND SINCE 2009. AM I TOO LATE? ISN'T IT BAD TO BUY THINGS AT THE TOP?

It's an injustice to Bitcoin to think of it like you were taught to think of the economy, finance, and money because bitcoin fixes the issues caused by those things (the legacy financial system).

Bitcoin's age is an indicator that you can never actually be too late. The price changes every day, so it's best to start buying when you can, as opposed to trying to wait and try to time the price. There is no top with Bitcoin because of the infinite nature of time.

I DON'T TRUST THE BANKS. I DON'T TRUST THE GOVERNMENT. I DON'T TRUST ANYBODY. LIFE IS AS GOOD AS IT'S GOING TO GET. WHY SHOULD I CARE ABOUT BITCOIN?

You're the perfect person for Bitcoin! Bitcoin is the money of enemies.

Bitcoin is a money run on a trust-less system. Historically, a major problem with money is the need to trust another party. Bitcoin solves that problem.

Bitcoin also teaches austerity. Transactions are final, and with the lighting network, instant. Bitcoin is scarce, you only spend sats on what you know you want at a price you respect or what is deemed correct by the merchant. Inventory priced in sats will be worth the sats or it will cost the merchant a bad reputation. Poor customer service or bad practices will cost the business owner business. Sat holders and spenders have the given right to speak with their money as opposed to exposing themselves, images and voices shouting, rating, and reviewing.

THE VENTURE CAPITALISTS, CORPORATIONS, WHITES, HISPANICS, AND ASIANS ALREADY HAVE A HOLDING ON MOST OF THE SUPPLY. I'M BLACK AND POOR. WHY SHOULD I CARE?

Bitcoin is a currency for all the people, most importantly the unbanked (poor). It's a free easy to set up nondiscriminatory bank account that you control. The point is for you to hold onto as much of it as you can now because its future value will be worth more.

There will always be someone with more something than you. All that matters is what you have and how you can capitalize what you have for more sats. Bitcoin takes away the middle man. In removing the middle man, Bitcoin enables direct to consumer spending anywhere in the world. People can choose who they want to support. Bitcoin gives you the freedom of financial choice.

You should care because who "they" say you are doesn't matter or mean anything when speaking with sats (bitcoin) because you're financially independent from them. The race that you identify as is nothing more than a tool for state economics. It is irrelevant to what you can afford. It's hard to understand because this is the first time since the sacrifice of Christ that all men are equally capable of holding their destiny without being tethered to the state.

BITCOIN IS AN OPEN-SOURCE CODE THAT ANYONE CAN COPY. WHY CAN'T SOMEBODY MAKE A BETTER BITCOIN? OR MAKE MORE BITCOIN?

Bitcoin is not the first of its kind. There has always been an "anti" state money group throughout the history of nations with government. Unfortunately, It wasn't until the introduction of the internet that the technology was available.

In 2009, Satoshi Nakamoto implemented a system that worked. It ran for a year and was mined cheaply until it was adopted as currency when exchanged for a pizza. The code is open source so that anyone who knows code can follow the code and recreate it to ensure that it continues to work; those are the alt-coins that can be assumed "cheaper" or "possibly better".

In actuality, they are copies of Bitcoin that solve specific technological issues. They are often run by self-interested company's or groups (centralized). They may work in specific use cases, but they definitely do not fix the money on the same level as Bitcoin, especially when Bitcoin is accompanied by the Lightning Network.

21 Million is all the Bitcoin that will ever be because trying to change that ultimately would be making a different currency altogether.

ONCE WE START TAKING BITCOIN LIKE WE TAKE CASH, THEN WE MIGHT AS WELL ACCEPT THE CHIP IN OUR ARM.

There are so many different arguments around this misconception but they are all distractions from the truth. Bitcoin being digital protects against violence in a way that current fiat money promotes and for a person who is tired of history's loop Bitcoin is the safest option.

Encryption allows for the protection of personal funds without the need of a biological host. Meaning computers can use bitcoin and people can use bitcoin but both are not mutually exclusive.

With Bitcoin as money, the likelihood of someone being forced to have a chip is highly unlikely. Bitcoin is a money of freedom. The very people who benefit from putting a chip in you are the very people bitcoin defunds.

WHY ARE BITCOINER'S MEAN ON TWITTER?

Bitcoin is a gift to the world. Satoshi Nakamoto made a sacrifice of fame, and wealth, to help the world fix its money problem. For centuries people have lost their lives at the expense of rich, elite, groups of people. In many cases, generations of families have coexisted in a world where their bodies are capital and profit potential.

Bitcoin makes life better and restores hope to a hopeless world. Therefore, it deserves to be defended. It deserves to be respected for the technology that it is.

It's an extreme disrespect to the selfless developers, engineers, and hodlers who have devoted their lives to preserving and strengthening the network when people of privilege and self-centered greed try and attack Bitcoin. Lies spread around Bitcoin hurt those that Bitcoin helps; that is unacceptable.

On Twitter, it is just tough love.

THE PROBLEM IS THE WAY WE VOTE. WE PICK THE WRONG POLITICIANS AND IN SOME CASES, DON'T EVEN VOTE AT ALL. THE PROBLEM ISN'T THE MONEY, IT'S US.

The money system is so corrupt that voting in some sense, can actually do more damage than good. A consequence of voting in the present for what impacts the future is the impact the stance has on those too young to understand the issue. For example, the fear of terroristic threats led America to enact the Patriot Act. Understandably, scared Americans gave up their rights in exchange for the feeling of safety. Unfortunately, time would reveal how destructive the "war on terror" was on the world.

The fear of terroristic threats killed soldiers and civilians. It wounded millions and left the world confused about who the good and bad parties were. Many have been disillusioned into believing things about people that destroyed relationships and reinforced stereotypes. Many were left having taken a stance on unvalidated facts spread as headlines. Interacting in public environments with people of different faiths was extremely difficult for so many because people were afraid. 20 years later, we all feel deserving of an apology.

Who benefits from war? Governments and their financiers; what do they have in common? Money—that's the problem.

WELCOME TO BITCOIN

I hosted a Bitcoin event
and it was a complete success.

No one showed up,
the one zoom caller left,
and while presenting
my mask kept rudely... interrupting.

The microphone crashed,
and I internally masked,
frustration of the food never arriving
fear
that everything all appeared to come from lack of preparing

That is the folly of pity, selfishness, and scarcity thinking.

FORE

I hosted a Bitcoin event
and it was an amazing blessing of a success.
I held the attention of all of my guests.
My little cousin, future in-laws, and aunts came.
My boyfriend stood strong,
We proved to make a really good team.

The pizza was late but
the party was
right on time.

The funny thing is
because of the event's success,

Anonymously

more people were fed
than the venue could've allowed
per Covid.

CHAPTER 5

BITCOIN'S BLACK AMERICAN EPIC

"When you spend your dollar out of the community in which you live the community in which you spend your dollar becomes richer and richer; the community out of which you take your money becomes poorer and poorer."

— Malcolm X

BIRTHED INTO THE lowest social status of one of the world's richest most influential countries and having multi-billion-dollar industries cultivated around "the culture" of blackness, the cries of black citizens fall on deaf ears. Instead of Black America gaining sympathy or receiving promised reparative aid, we receive confused criticisms, mainstream media speculation, and talking heads debating justification of our treatment.

The lack of compassion, respect, and support is further perpetuated by the opinions of body-less beings on the internet, specifically, those famously celebrated on social media. There will always be pros and cons to everything: the internet is a technology that exploded unto the world and transformed learning and the human experience greatly. Social networking sites have been beneficial in creating a space for black enterprises to thrive—it has also been incredibly dangerous. The very algorithms that are designed to help our businesses also allow white supremacist institutions to ensure that black America represents itself as spoiled, ignorant, distracted people. Justifying the laissez-faire attitude, other Americans (and the rest of the world) watch American blacks being tried, convicted, and executed in the street as content.

The treatment of 21st century black Americans as they exercised their rights to protest the murders of George Floyd, Rayshard Brooks, and Brionna Taylor in 2020 revealed just how undervalued black people are to the nation we call home. The destruction caused by police, anti-black organizations, and the media to incite violence and confusion put conscious individuals in the mindset of 1938 Germany at the dawn of the second world war, Kristallnacht.

Late November 9th early November 10th, the Germans destroyed and looted businesses in the Jewish district under the protection of the German government. The Nazi regime decided German Jews would not be considered citizens. This comparison suggests Black America is heading for war. Mainstream media will insist there is no threat. Some outlets may report the war to be between blacks and the police, the fascist vs. antifascist, racist vs. anti-racist, white supremacy vs. liberalism, all distractions but none the enemy. Black America is at war with the American financial system.

The use of social networking sites and mainstream media revenue strategies has subconsciously conditioned Black Americans to apathetically relate to their blackness. Simultaneously, Black Americans are choosing not to think for ourselves. A consequence of the conditioning is black Americans not acting or making choices that are in the best interest of the black community. Instead, we allow political organizations and wealthy influencers to monetize and gain notoriety from the exploitation of black trauma. This practice of controlling and manipulating the way blacks think is not new; the use of social networks to do it is.

In his book, *Powernomics: An Economic Plan for Black America,* Dr. Claud Anderson articulates that Black America was brought here to be the free labor class of America. The book urges Black America to work together and act as a country within a country, harnessing our skin, our blackness, as Black America's identifier. He teaches failing to do so will result in Black America forever remaining America's permanent underclass. Dr. Anderson argues that black Americans have never truly been emancipated and that the reparations we are asking for is more than the government could dream of repaying.

Dr. Anderson is not wrong; essentially Black Americans have been bringing daisies to a gunfight every time we protest or ask and wait for reparations. The only way for black America to win the war is to work together as a collective and ethno aggregate. Dr. Anderson dedicates his life to writing books that reveal truths and strategies for Black America to acquire wealth. A black American historian and educator Dr. Anderson witnessed the black excellence that segregation afforded blacks as well as how the civil rights movement burdened Black America.

The Powernomic strategy discusses a five-story building model aimed at black empowerment and wealth-building via education, ownership and black enterprise. Each building level represents a task of ownership that Black Americans must accomplish in order to ethnoaggregate successfully. The building, intentional in its design, was erected vertically to represent black America's upward progression. Dr. Claud Anderson envisioned his strategy to have been implemented by 2005. Instead, Black Americans would be devastated by the globally destructive collapse of the American housing market in 2008[11].

The only good thing to come from the housing market collapse of 2008, was Bitcoin in 2009. Satoshi Nakamoto, a pseudo-anonymous cypherpunk, published the Bitcoin White Paper[12], a decentralized peer to peer digital currency, a solution to the world's Byzantine General problem, in protest of the banks receiving bailouts and bonuses. The white paper discusses a new currency, Bitcoin, it was created to allow the world's unbanked to control their wealth. In other words, the unbanked become their own bank. This revolutionary

---

11   Anderson, Claud. Black Labor, White Wealth: The Search for Power and Economic Justice. Duncan & Duncan, 1994.
12   Nakamoto, Satoshi. "Bitcoin: A Peer-to-Peer Electronic Cash System." *Bitcoin.pdf*, Satoshin@Gmx.com, 31 Oct. 2008, bitcoin.org.

technology, a hard sound money, will ultimately change the way in which wealth is distributed around the globe.

Black America is the lowest-ranked social class in the American hierarchy. America is known to be a wealthy superpower that welcomes immigrants and refugees across the world with tax incentives. For Black America, the country is very cruel. Black America is America's overlooked unbanked. This is intentional.

UCI Law Professor Mehrsa Baradaran uncovers the intentional destruction of the black banking sector in her book, *The Color of Money: Black Banks and the Racial Wealth Gap*. She explains how despite black resilience the racist white infrastructure impeded black banking with every economic depression. The black bank competitors and investors that destroyed and stole from black citizens would ultimately become beneficiaries of American citizens' bailout in 2008.

Bitcoin was created for the unbanked. Therefore, Bitcoin is being argued as essential for black American survival. If Black Americans work together and ethno-aggregate on the Bitcoin network Black America will liberate itself while simultaneously defunding a white supremacist system. The same system that continues to enslave and exploit black American people today.

In the famous Bitcoin white paper, Satoshi Nakamoto discusses problems Bitcoin solves with the global financial system. Bitcoin is extremely powerful because it eliminates the violent, thieving despot, the middle man. The technology provides security from confiscation, it also offers the world a truly scarce asset class that will redistribute the world's wealth with its scarcity and distribution schedule. Nakamoto's solution to a complex computer science problem, the Byzantine General's problem, also solves the problems of white supremacy by dismantling the racist institutions that support Black America's underclass status. Bitcoin ultimately validates Dr. Claud Anderson's economic plan.

Bitcoin had not yet been coded when Dr. Anderson published Powernomics. It was not until American tax payers were forced to bail out the banking institutions that stole from them and created the global financial crisis of 2008 that Satoshi Nakamoto was compelled to destroy the currency we are all currently dying for. It was the American Government's blatant disregard for humanity that yielded Bitcoin's release to the public.

Black Americans can grow to see Satoshi Nakamoto as inspiration for breaking free of a corrupt system that continues to oppress us and benefit financially from black post-traumatic stress from that oppression. Bitcoin is young, but it is old enough to act as a responsible option to choose for the currency of Black America. Not only is it a currency by definition, it is scarce, fungible, portable, divisible, and verifiable. Bitcoin possesses all the properties that make it a better asset and less risky than the USD. Eventually, the currency of Black American people will be Bitcoin because the currency of the world will be Bitcoin. Since it is still early in the age of Bitcoin adoption, Black America has time to liberate itself and increase purchasing power. By increasing our spending power and earning potential we are simultaneously redefining and re-establishing what Blackness means to the world.

Before we can employ the Bitcoin Strategy for Black Liberation, there must be the understanding that as a collective our mindset and lifestyles must change. We can no longer desire the things that do not empower us to grow and leave behind a legacy. The battle has lasted so long the only way to win the war is to completely shed ourselves of the "blackness" that has been forced on us like armor. It is time we take responsibility and choose to define our people for ourselves. We must strategically move and act cohesively.

As a black American (or ally) a choice has to be made. There is a choice between being who you choose to be or being who the state has labeled you. For example, the state labeled my cousin, criminal. This label made him unable to serve his country, unable to act and move freely, and forced him to focus on living a life of constant struggle. Bitcoin does away with oppressive labels. By owning and stacking satoshi, my cousin is able to think for himself and spend his earnings freely.

Bitcoin allows my cousin and others, to have the freedom to choose how he serves his community. My cousin is no longer defined by his past. Instead, he is an entrepreneur who solves problems for his community with the business he owns. He is a father who can be proud of himself and the choices he has made for his future.

Bitcoin encourages and empowers us to take responsibility for our time, it enables us to start living intentionally. For those encouraged to ethno-aggregate and be empowered by Bitcoin, the first part of the strategy is changing your mindset, the second step is manifesting the change by leveraging your belongings for bitcoin. The first level of the Powernomic building challenges Black America to own what we produce, consume, and trade. This is the beginning of ethnoaggregating with Bitcoin. At this level, black Americans use bitcoin to purchase the products that we need to live. We create the solutions to the problems that are plaguing black people in America. It is here where we rebuild trust with one another by tipping and patronizing other blacks in Satoshi (sats). We need to amass as many sats as we can individually and collectively. The tipping function on Twitter is a great way to start!

Leveraging belongings for bitcoin means selling items or possessions that have no utility/purpose and using the return to purchase sats. Leveraging is simply getting rid of everything that was purchased because it was cute, on-trend, or designer and choosing to buy things that can be used to help progress your life or make it easier. If it is valuable but purposeless, sell it and buy bitcoin. Cut all unnecessary expenses. This is the beginning of "downsize" and "downgrade" mentality. If the house is too big or too much, downsize. The goal is to buy as many sats as possible. Having multiple wallets labeled for different occasions will help with organization. The most secure wallet being the reservoir long-term holding (minimum 7 years). The other wallets are needed for transacting with Black businesses and allies around the world. Black America needs five things right now: multiple streams of income, shelter, transportation, nutrition, and Bitcoin. We are at war.

Be deliberate; instead of quitting the job, use it to finance the rebellion for however long you can stand it. Let the "job" give you the cash that is spent on bills, the government, and services provided by non-blacks. If it's a service or product that is sold by a Black American then use Satoshis (the currency of Black America) to buy it. Any business that accepts Bitcoin is considered an ally; spend your sats with them.

Donate to black churches, patronize non-profit organizations, etc. with satoshi. Solve problems that arise in your everyday life or community by developing business plans and executing them. Work together with like-minded thinkers and form companies that will eventually become industries. Allow your creativity to create opportunities for you to earn satoshi and help grow the community. Pick up a hobby and/or learn a new skillset. Black America will need tradespeople. Farmers, coders, housekeepers, mechanics, welders, HVAC, plumbers, etc. are all needed in the community. As ethnoaggregating on the network becomes a part of the Black American lifestyle, black-owned counseling services, clinics, and community programs will be better funded to fulfill their missions. Volunteering, giving honest, constructive feedback and community engagement will help Black Americans earn and grow and regain trust in one another. It is best to think of level one like you would when developing a new habit. Start with trying it for 7 days, then 14, then 21, then 45 days finally, after 90 days it becomes a lifestyle. It is during this time that a life strategy should be developed for yourself and your family. Test it out by gifting friends, children, colleagues with sats instead of cards, chocolates, etc.

The second level of the five-story building challenges black Americans to amass enough wealth that we are capable of purchasing the loyalty and allegiance of politicians. Acquiring politicians ensures that we have representatives who are employed to create a policy that is beneficial to Black America. This level ensures black America has the freedom to conduct business with countries that are aligned with perpetuating black empowerment. This allows us the opportunity to strengthen global relations through travel and trading with countries that accept bitcoin[13].

In June 2021, President Nayib Bukele made Bitcoin legal tender for El Salvador, Central America's smallest, most densely populated country. Jorge Valenzuela and Mike Peterson first introduced bitcoin through a community project, Bitcoin Beach in 2019. Three years later, El Salvador is the world's frontrunner in employing bitcoin as legal tender.

Bitcoin Beach is a project aimed at fulfilling the needs of the youth in El Zonte, a poor surfing town in El Salvador. The project began with an anonymous donation of 1 bitcoin and a promise not to convert the donation into USD. Mike Peterson (with the help of others) introduced El Zonte to bitcoin and the Lightning Network. This partnership led to the El Zonte project being named Bitcoin Beach.

---

13   Anderson, Claud. PowerNomics®: The National Plan to Empower Black America. PowerNomics Corp. of America, 2001.

Along with a circular economy, Bitcoin Beach created an atmosphere in which young children suffering from the social and economic traumas of poverty, such as fatherlessness and gang affiliation, can own bitcoin and have autonomy over their socioeconomic trajectory. Jorge Valenzuela, Mike Peterson, and the youth of El Zonte gained the attention of Jack Mallers, CEO of Zap Labs/Lightning Strike and El Salvador's forward focused President, Nayib Bukele. Ultimately, their hard work would lead to President Bukele making bitcoin legal tender for the country. El Salvador and the youth of Bitcoin Beach have forged a path for Black America to follow. By enacting a circular economy with bitcoin as currency, Black America will be able to have autonomy over its socioeconomic trajectory as well.

EL Zonte, El Salvador saw a 50% decline in crime with the implementation of bitcoin as the currency of Bitcoin Beach. The monetary network restored hope to a country misjudged and overlooked by the rest of the world, something that impoverished people around the world share. Bitcoin is safe money, free of government corruption and volatility, and solves global problems caused by the central banking system. It empowered citizens of El Zonte, El Salvador to convince President Bukele to introduce Bitcoin as the nation's second currency. President Bukele is excited to see what the future brings for a country riddled with an impoverished and hopeless past.

The Black American community has evolved congruently with America as a nation. Blacks have participated in the major

American wars as well as contributed to making America a thriving nation. Before America became an immigrant paradise, it was a fledgling European colony in need of cheap labor. The first Africans were not brought over as "inhuman savages" but indentured servants with limited freedoms and the hope of greater autonomy in the future. This changed in the mid-17th century when white male elites learned about interracial marriage—a union between white female servants and black male servants would grant Black men the ability to vote and participate in America's growing economy. Over time, with the institution of slavery, fear of retaliation for forced black enslavement provoked the passage of legislation that stripped Black bodies of all autonomy.

Slave rebellions broke out for decades. Each rebellion provided an opportunity for the ruling class to psychologically intimidate the enslaved class into fearful submissiveness by means of violence and public execution. Meritorious manumission, a practice where freedom was granted to those who warned whites about suspected slave insurrections, engendered distrust amongst enslaved Americans. This distrust evolved into an involuntary reflex within Black Americans that has continued to modern times.

The American Civil War was a transitional period in America's history in which, for a short while after it, Blacks were allowed limited participation in the Government. We were also granted permission to learn how to read, write, and earn wages. This Black freedom, unfortunately, led to retaliation in the form of unending psychological torture through centuries of lynchings, murders, and disappearances. In response, Black cities began to pop up around the nation. These Black communities provided security, protection, healthcare, education, and employment for Black Americans. As a result, Black American culture (currently Black America's primary export) was introduced to the wider society via prolific writers, scholars, and entertainers. Black owned banks, transportation services, and universities thrived, although under constant threat of destruction at the hands of the Klan or defunding at the whim of the State. Nonetheless, a vibrant Black circular economy was established similar to that of the Irish, Jewish, Dutch, and Italian immigrants (referred to as White Americans today). Unfortunately, Black American circular economies would end in massacres or political piracy unlike the Jewish, Irish, and Italian immigrants.

The current monetary network is a top-down system built on top of the internet. Each method of payment has its own monetary network: Visa, PayPal, Venmo, CashApp, Zelle, the banking apps, etc. These networks are plugged into banks' ledgers (accounts) to validate transactions (and solve any disputes) between the seller and buyer. Validations ensure the purchaser has the funds to settle the payment. This process is flawed, slow, and expensive. Depending on the network, some disputes may take weeks to finalize. Chargebacks and merchant disputes also cost Black entrepreneurs time and revenue. These are not issues with Bitcoin.

There is also an addition to Bitcoin called the Lightning Network. Lightning makes financial transactions easier than the current payment system being used. The Lightning Network finalizes transactions across international borders within a few seconds. It opens channels on the Bitcoin blockchain that enable multiple disputes to be settled with finality in less time than the traditional system. The Lightning Wallet App, Strike, enables users to convert between currencies seamlessly. For Black Americans and Salvadorans, the wallet seamlessly converts USD to Bitcoin and vice versa, which means they can use USD when necessary. Users can also store their wealth in Bitcoin. They are able to utilize the strike app for transactions along with traditional mediums of cold storage for long-term savings.

Prior to proposing the legislation that makes Bitcoin legal tender in El Salvador, President Bukele took a firm stance on "crypto". El Salvador made ICOs (initial coin offerings) illegal. President Bukele understood the dangers associated with centralized tech projects commonly called *cryptocurrencies* or *alt-coins (shitcoins)*: they are volatile and serve no real purpose in alleviating poverty or reducing crime. He saw past the flat get-rich-quick promises and understood the devastating chaotic volatility of the crypto market and how it could impact Salvadorans.

Bitcoin is not a cryptocurrency, but a hard digital asset. This distinction is crucial to preserving what little wealth the impoverished Salvadorans have amassed. In 2022, the IMF targeted Bukele for his Bitcoin position. Bukele doubled down by increasing his holding and using the dip in Bitcoin's price as a *sale on sats*.

President Bukele is an example of the positioning we should all take. Buy, hold, transact, hold, and buy some more.

Many Black Americans do not have bank accounts or even meet the financial requirements to maintain an account with a bank. In fact, poverty throughout the world leaves entire demographics of oppressed people like the people of El Salvador and Black America unbanked. With Bitcoin, business owners, community leaders, and anyone interested are able to run their own nodes and verify the transactions on the blockchain themselves. When used in conjunction with the Lightning Network, the Bitcoin monetary network protects both the merchant and the buyer, a luxury Black Americans serving Black America can seldomly afford.

Rebuilding a Black economy allows Black youth to work for more than debt repayment. Black youth are inundated with fearmongering propaganda, offering them little more than a life of servitude via student loan debt, the legacy corporate sector, or the military. Black youth are empowered by Bitcoin to create generational wealth for a future that is different from their parents. Bitcoin Beach has shown the world how Bitcoin empowers the youth to pursue trades, rebuild the community and keep it safe and clean. There is no better group of people equipped to tend to the needs of Black America than Black Americans.

El Salvador was once reported as the world's most violent country. An American-funded civil war left Salvadorans seeking asylum in countries throughout the 1970s and 80s, decimating the country's population. What's more, the arrival of American prison/street gangs contributed to the high crime rate. These gangs (MS13 and Barrio 18) formed to help Salvadoran immigrants living in gang ridden California. Unfortunately, gang culture would spill into El Salvador after members were deported from America. Gang violence created a poor, fatherless generation of Salvadoran youth with limited options and no ability to build generational wealth in the future. Imagine what a Bitcoin based community could do for the neighborhoods of Chicago? Atlanta? Or Detroit?

Bitcoin Beach organizer Jorge Valenzuela started Bitcoin Beach's circular economy in an attempt to solve problems associated with fatherlessness in El Zonte, El Salvador. Bitcoin Beach's circular economy enabled the children of the incarcerated, murdered, and/or gang-affiliated opportunities to afford education and a good quality of life within El Salvador. They no longer have to lower themselves to refugees status to make a living. Their protection comes from having a hard currency to use and save instead of seeking protection from gang affiliation. The youth of Black America deserve similar opportunities.

If Black America's community leaders and business owners chose to follow Jorge's example and use Bitcoin to start a circular economy, Black youth would be encouraged to restore trust and empathy within their local communities. Black youth would have the opportunity to own and operate hospitals, restaurants, grocery stores, farms, technology firms, engineering firms, etc., and solve problems plaguing the Black community. President Bukele said that "a community can benefit from Bitcoin," and the Black American community is in dire need of Bitcoin's benefits. With the empowerment Bitcoin provides, community programs, like the 22 programs in El Zonte, can be organized in Black America to restore hope to a people who have been terrorized into hopelessness.

We will be encouraged to establish relations with countries of the diaspora and other oppressed people across the globe. This will be done most effectively after Black Americans return to the "hood". We no longer have black communities. There are no longer neighborhoods situated around black hospitals, grocery stores, pharmacies, transportation companies, etc. established to meet the needs of Black America. Moving back to the "hood" with bitcoin as our currency will empower us to gentrify our own communities creating safe havens for blackness, and the raising of black children.

Dr. Anderson suggests black America's owning of politicians will allow us to influence the justice system. This is the most important element of the building in that the justice system is responsible for the mass incarceration of black men; the phone recorded murders of unarmed black people in the streets, and the extinction of the black nuclear family. By having ownership of the politicians that represent black America, we the black people, establish laws that protect us from the oppressors. With Bitcoin being the currency of Black America, Black Americans can speak without fear of retribution. Black America working as a collective on the bitcoin network ultimately boost trust in the currency globally and creates a stronger network effect. This makes non-black bitcoiners our allies. This allows Black America to become extremely competitive on a global stage.

The fourth level of the building urges black America to own the media so that we control and promote our culture and enterprises. It is at this level that the work contributed by black coders, programmers, and developers on Bitcoin core, the bitcoin open-source software, can provide evidence to the world that Black America was forced into an underclass status by the white supremacist ideology underwriting the public policy of the American government. The same American government that helped liberate the Jews and paid restitution to the natives, Panamanians, and Japanese; forced its own citizens into financial enslavement and perpetuated lies about them to avoid taking responsibility for centuries of oppression and domestic terrorism.

As a people, we can utilize Bitcoin's technology as an innovation that empowers us to liberate ourselves from the state and its industries. The industries black America builds as a nation within a nation will be the direct result of liberation with bitcoin. The truth about Blackness will be exported alongside other black-owned goods and services.

The final level of the five-story building is education. Black America will possess enough wealth that we no longer have to teach our children how to survive. Our children are no longer forced to live under the labels given to them by a racist institution. Instead, we educate our children on how to thrive, how to embrace their blackness, and how to live unapologetically with purpose. This strategy once implemented, will promote positive blackness and reinforce the core principles of black liberation: self-sufficiency, honesty, justice, loyalty, and family.

Bitcoin empowers black America to liberate itself and proliferate because Bitcoin incentivizes the nuclear family. It incentivizes thriftiness and self- sovereignty. In a Bitcoin planet, we can be content and happy in our lives. We can create a life for ourselves where we can live fully and unabashedly. Bitcoin empowers Black America to protest the state that has been terrorizing us domestically for half a millennia.

Black America holding the keys to our bitcoin will allow us to reintroduce ourselves and our customs to the world. We can re-establish how important black culture and melanated people are and have been to the world. Bitcoin provides black people with tangible options instead of empty promises and government programs. We are no longer forced to subscribe to stereotypes and arguments over racism, colorism, sexism, fascism, and any other distraction that's trending on social media or in the mainstream media.

IF WE REALLY WANT TO WIN AND END THE WAR, BLACK AMERICA NEEDS BITCOIN.

CHAPTER 6
A BLACK AMERICAN ORATORY

"We are poetry. And poetry is us. Those who share with us are poetry. Those who sit and eat our pig feet and chitterlings and those who come on Sunday to worship with us. "
— Nikki Giovanni
Make Me Rain

SOCIAL GRACES

Let it not be mistaken,
every civilization
has social graces.

Courteous behavior
that makes
everyday
bearable.

It's common place
to think
the things people say
have meaning but hold no merit.

Words are expensive
and
should never be taken for granted.

We have responsibility
to one another
to consider each other
human
seek
And
maintain peace.

For morality
is personal choice
forcing
good people
to use their voice
stand strong
fight,
deliberately combat evil.

A choice made to disturb the dismal
darkness
that looms over the earth.

How?

With light,
all it takes is a twinkle.

BROKEN ENGLISH

We speak in Cliches
So the words we say

Have no meaning

Every syllable an act of avoiding
Speaking vaguely
Never taking
Accountability
For the way that
Others understand
The intention behind the words mentioned during
uncomfortable discussions.

Ultimately,
We are all afraid
to listen.

METAMEDIA

Momma called it the devil,
and she didn't wanna be on it.

High school classmates needed to include her,
send info about
the
reunion.

Now,
Tina Johnson
is on Facebook.

An account so private,
her body now ashes and
I still can't see what gets posted to it.

I'm not your friend; I'm your mother.
In real-life and
whatever virtual one.

The purpose of this rhyme
is not to be
nostalgic
or look back in time.

This is me calling social media
the anti-Christ

ASCENDANCY

The developers
at
Instagram say,
I
am
a
verified
star.

Pale blue will forever be my color.
1 Million followers,
you can refer to me as
influencer.

A number that is only there to remind us just how popular
we aren't.

REVELATION

I wrestle with hatred of self;
a feeling disconnected from my soul.

Therefore,

this is a
revelation.

BLACK LIKE ME

Why must I turn on the TV and see
another woman,
black like me
stolen, beaten, cheated,
addicted.

Why must we be garbage?
Is that what the media wants us to believe
about ourselves?
Is that the narrative,
still?

It is the women,
who are black like me
that are currently,
and have been,
succeeding.

Black men long quit,
forced into submission,
Or else it's plain negligence.
White men have historically been
corrupt.
While white women know just enough to be victims
of situation

and circumstance.
Immigrants can't count this time,
for they are white
according to what has already been ratified.

We, black American women are succeeding.
Have been.
Yet,
the media and entertainment industry uses
spin
to condition
strong black women
into thinking
we are only good enough to be kidnapped, sold, and fed dope.

SKIN

What is pretty?

Who decides?

Is it light eyes and shy smiles?
Blonde hair, see-through thighs?
3B curls? Latin spice?

Why do I constantly compare myself to that?
To her?
Because of him?

The one that I want
doesn't want me,
why?

Skin

PRIVILEGE

Nobody wants to be a racist.
They just enjoy doing racist shit.

Holding onto privilege as if it were
a light jacket
packed away by Mother in a grade school bookbag.

Using drugs, stealing clothes, enjoying
the rush of getting away with it.

Adrenaline pumping,
tears falling,
calling daddy.

Lawyer makes sure
it's probation
soon as he meets with
lady justice.

WORKING WITH WHITE WOMEN

Never in my life have I ever felt like this,
Scratch that I gotta make sure I spell that like d-i-S
Only because that's what's expected, I say.

It doesn't matter how well I articulate or enunciate

To you, I'm deserving of nothing more than the thought you
        think.
Preconceived notions of the person I am because of the skin
        I wear.
You should be ashamed of yourself,
How high you keep your nose in the air.

You are ignorant, naive, with such egregious behavior,
Yet the world allows you to call yourself, professional.
Professionally unprofessional
Exceptionally pathetic.

CAN'T STOP WON'T QUIT

Not being white is a problem
Only to white people.
There's power in melanin.
To have black skin means more than the socialized themes
Of Niggers Hanging on the corner at midnight
Or Little Nigger girls with their fat asses and gum popping
    fingernail snapping
head patting hoe behavior.
No, that's not being black at all.
When you've got that extra fattening melanin, not fattening
    like bad but fattening like, "that sho'le taste good" fat
    back in Collards fattening.
When you've got that melanin baby,
You've got a power to run the world and a history screaming
    you better not stop.
And that's why they hate. That's what they don't like.
They don't like that when you look back
On the history, they wrote and realize
How often they show weakness
When you look back at the history we made.
The history we're making
And the future we have.
Do you understand beautiful brown child, why they hate you?
They dislike you because you're a reminder that they can't
    stop you.

You will be more
have more and
do better than they have.

DEATH X 1M CUTS

I carry this burlap teddy bear
filled with razors to remind myself
I am alive.

Every night I nuzzle up to pain
hold it
crying.
With every squeeze
metal stabs beyond my flesh into my bone
revealing
thick hot liquid
pumping through heart ventricles
into lungs.

Every day I awaken in agony
pain is only felt when the wounds begin to heal.

I squeeze harder.
Cut deeper.
Hoping to reopen, enlarge, and
deepen each cut
desperate attempts of easing pain towards
relief.

When will I outgrow this?

When will I love myself more than this
Tetanus ridden sack of misery?

When will blood stained clothes
act as enough reminder
of my
pain.

When will I choose Jesus
and ask for his strength to heal?

CHOPIN

Hush,
Quietly inhale
tickling salty vapor

water crashes against rock
An act of violence

Angry aggressive agitated
waves
create calm chaotic peace within earth's soma.

Exhale
energy transfers pain outwardly
into the abysmal darkness of the sea

DEPROGRAM US

Deprogram us.

Change the way we see ourselves
force a collective reconstruction of our identity.
Erase the negativity.
Our lenses were given to us
and
they are all
filthy.

Blonde
ginger
brown
silk like hair,
thigh gaps,
rosy cheeks.

Effortlessly gorgeous
and
white.
Skin
the beauty standard of
perfection.
Beautiful black celebrity faces
smile

and hide
the pain
of the
industry executives
entertainment fans
and critics
Saying, "you're no Marilyn."

MIRRORS

I wish I saw beauty reflected in the mirror.
I wish I saw a gorgeous face
Attached to an impeccable smile.

A delicate nose
proportionate
to button up eyes.

Perfection and an even complexion.

If not for Instagram
I'd have never known
just how many perfect specimens
roam the globe.

TWITTER

One Summer,
I felt prolific
and took to Twitter.

By Winter,
I became angry,
insecure,

Disconnected
from society's
graces;

I stepped away from the computer,

Self-righteous.

FORGIVE YOURSELF

Girl, stop.
I'm good on all this.
My voice is hoarse from the stress of demanding you
    understand,
I am sorry.

My only intention was to be supportive.
Honest
and
Genuine.

It is fine.
Don't even think about it.
Especially,
not now.

I've cried,
and forgotten the issue.
You no longer have lies to tell.

Or,
did you realize
I've given this over to GOD.
All is well.

Speaking with tear-filled eyes
arguing to apologize
nothing more than a waste of time.

Only thing left to do is move along.

All of this advice
I continuously give myself.

MORE ADVICE TO SELF

Don't go there!
Stop, my darling girl

DO NOT
compare yourself to others.

Your gifts are yours, and because of that
there will never be another.

Kind, honest, and graceful.

Your confidence is noticeable
clothes are always tasteful.
You govern yourself with tact.

You have an opinion,
you articulate
genuine.

GOD has designed him
for
you.

DO NOT
go looking

no need for searching.

Your one is out there
Praying for
you.

RELATIONS

Friendship is simple,
people are difficult.
Relationships are easy or they should be.

A relationship's level of difficulty
its depth and robustness
are completely dependent on the willingness of the
   transactor.

Acceptance, understanding,
compassion, empathy
all
attributes of a good friendship.

Selfless love,
neither arrogant nor contrite,
That is the single greatest entity.

Love is the only thing
humans need
from
other human beings.

PUBLIC EDUCATION

History books are tools
used by public schools
to perpetuate white propaganda.

Bureaucratic systematics
bigoted tactics placed children
within pre-outlined margins

as goes every American epic.

The racist comes out the victim
and their mother
blameless.

All while the accused beg,
And
dream.

They dream big dreams
because they have no shot at a future.

A career, benign,
maybe
9-5
big city or small town

a life defined as regular with average debts.

QUEEN-ISH

Black woman,
take pride in yourself.

Have a bit more tact and class.
Stop.

Everytime you step out shouldn't yield
opportunity to show your ass.
Be a little quieter,
take notice and reflect.
Stop being quick to combatively interject.

Someone told you that was cute.
Them niggas gassin you up like
the moves you make
are the right ones to choose.
Let's see which one leads you to love
or—genuine respect.
Instead of using your body
for finding pleasure and
avoiding regret.
Get a life, go.
Create your own wealth.
Quit seeking validation from
feelings of

warmth or
worse,
male pseudo security.
You hate yourself.
You seek attention as validation
find inner peace darling.
There is nothing better than it.

UNFORTUNATELY

No matter how hard you work
or
long you stride
to them...

you will never leave the seat assigned.

You could have millions and live on the highest
hill
within the top
tax bracket

you will be nothing
more
than what they've already decided.

A ratchet
pathetic
being
deserving enslavement.

physical chains
shackles
no longer exist
dehumanizing weights key locked onto brown wrists.

But
social places
they created
for us
should be good enough
as to remain commensurable to theirs.

DEMOCRACY

The only lives protected
Are white men and pedophiles

I get it
When the constitution was written
The only bodies that were counted
Voted
privilege.
Must not forget to mention the reiteration
Found in most congregations' book with the white Jesus.

Images of the idolized
control the media
White face
Dictates what the populace love and hate
They
Harnessed the power stolen from the powerful
Destroying what is good and blessed
Recreating complete hatred
Again and again
Generation upon generation
The same fight across the nation.

Majority rule minorities die.
Or they are jailed, imprisoned

Human beings becoming psychosocial experiments.
Test subjects
While white women and their new found freedom aide in
    elitism
The white woman comes complete with a stage to watch her
    shiny hair and dull blue eyes cry.

American beauties with sunken faces
are given space and always shown societal grace
to be
"Under" worked or underpaid.
Sexually harassed
Front desk maids, madams, secretary's
Seeks professional advice from CEO's and Presidents
    avoiding commitments
And happy to help young blonde get ahead

We empower the imposters.

By reinforcing their behaviors with agreement and
    deflection.

PATIENCE

You need to be still.
That's a mountain, not a hill.
You can't just decide to climb it.

Torches, oil rigs, railways,
cataclysmic catastrophes concern everyone
in an explosion's wake.
Rubble, smoke, carcinogens
make breathless air.

Proximal distance to destruction
leaves large debris
scattered along miles.

DEATH OF A PARENT

There is something infinitely humbling about losing a parent,
some
consume themselves with avoidance,
others
bargain against reality,
many
mourn loudly while minor resentments against heaven
        silently build in their hearts,
few
morph into pseudo piety in search of meaning and answers,
some
fall gracefully into darkness
dark rooms,
dark moods,
dark humor

all
An emotional consequence of human—selfishness
for death is only sad when the dying won't rise again.

When they didn't accept the promise.
and
absolutely nobody
is currently praying for them.
Or

Their soul...
that is sad.

That is sad for while the living grieves the dying
they are also dead themselves,
then there is nothing done that is saving anyone...
all because of selfishness?

Life is more than self fore
we were not created to live for ourselves
or along with the guidelines of the world... who is the world?

Governments. Regulators. Authoritative Dictators.
Those who decide what's best for you without knowing your
    name.

They tell you how to grieve because your grief is their profit.
Living how they want feels good to you but it is the state that
    has revenue to gain.
They tell you when it is acceptable to move forward
They tell you what's the next step to take.
Because their time
is what your life depends on.

Be free.

Death of every kind is about the rebirth

The afterlife —when you return to the creator.

Death is life when you love as you are told.

Death is life when you know
The creator promises your creation with love
there is a promise that your love is
real in JESUS.

Pray while you mourn so your grief won't be hard to bear.
Pray while you cry so your eyes will be washed
clear.

Be purposeful amongst the living
and deliberate with your time.

For death is not about the dying
it's about the afterlife.

MINUSCULE STEPS

You don't just outgrow bad habits.
There must be conscious effort to be
Whomever it is you will be happy,
Content and grateful being.

There will come time to move forward.
Rest
until you have the strength
to pick up a leg
then
pick up the other

Teedle
toddle
Step
Forward.

W?

What is fear?

Failure. Destruction.

What are you afraid of?

Destruction.

Destruction of?

Possibility.

When would possibility be destroyed?

Consciousness.

How do you attain consciousness?

Quest yielding answers.

Who gives the answers to the questions?

GOD

therefore, be careful what you ask.

Where will fear of consciousness lead you?

Nowhere.

CHAPTER 7

TRANSITIONING DISCERNMENT

"I have been in Sorrow's kitchen and licked out all the pots. Then I have stood on the peaky mountain wrapped in rainbows, with a harp and sword in my hands."

— Zora Neale Hurston

THE TIME TO REFLECT

Wind pressing firmly against my ear
tickling angelic kisses
from loved one's past.
Reminders they are always near.
I take comfort in solace
silence, still.

Time alone is sacred.

DATING

I tell you who I am;
you look me in my face
and see
what you want.

My mouth forms words that dare and speak truth.

You look past my honesty,
strength, and confidence
to gaze at my
smile.

THANKS LADY

I love you Grandmama,
I do.
You taught me to be a lady.
a prayerful,
graceful,
agreeable
lady.
While you're in all ways
always
a Queen.

ONLY CHILD SYNDROME

I remember
playing school-house.
Grandmama's stuffed "babies" were my pupils.

Running off to class on Monday
only to lie about my Saturdays and Sundays.

I had a strict mother.

I understand her love and I am secure in it.
Thanks Mom.

Weekends were always Granma's house
until a point
then they became
weekend getaways, shopping trips, and family-time
minus a live-in father and siblings.

PROCEED WITH CAUTION

Your sex is yours.
Do with it as you please.
BEWARE!
Each time will yield its own consequence.

Make each transaction
calculated
instead of living in fantasy
you will realize your power
to choose,
to fight,
to speak up for yourself.

DO NOT HATE

LOVE,
seek, question,
and

find.

When you don't live in
hatred,
you forget about forgetting.

The people, the behavior,
the hurt dissipates
acceptance remains
forgiving
understanding
then
choosing to leave
them
right where
they
are.

Doing so
sustains your peace,
cleanses your heart and helps you move
forward.

Whatever you decide,
think first
be responsible.
Human is not your master
Human is a character in the chapter book of earthly life.

Human contribution,
a juicy detail,
a blippet,
short sentence,
full paragraph.

Doesn't matter!

Every action has its accompanying consequence.
BE WARNED.

OLD FASHIONED

Love

I've never been in love before
I think I've only loved.

I loved the way they treated me.
I loved the way they made me feel.
I loved that when I was with them, my past was never real.
I loved how loving them would always turn into more...
A sexual relationship, security, and fun.
Movie dates, staying up late, someone new to explore.
Every time I've loved I dreamt of having what I'd never seen
    my mother have before.

All that I know about love has been passed down, American
    folklore.
The first time I recall hearing the word, of course, came from
    my mother. She kissed my cheek every morning, "I love
    ya, have a good day."
My grandma first told me the story.
Oh, she loved herself some Johnson now...
mmm mm He was tall, good lookin, and "dahhwk huhney". —
"He was about somethin' too." (I still chuckle at the way she
    talked about her husband.)

A seaman in the Navy,
That looked damn good in dress Blues.
He complimented her smile, her eyes, and her fashion
ability's, too. She was a classy lady
sophisticated;
She waited to kiss.
They'd later get married
And travel the world.
1 house and 6 kids,
then the marriage ended with his murder.

A church going woman,
Sharp dressed and attractive.
As time moved forward, another story of love would be told.
It started when Grandma met the first reverend.
Lowe of Albany, Georgia.
And oh my, did she love him.

I loved him too. He was the grandfather that I really knew.
A jolly old man full of laughter, wisdom, peppermint hugs,
and intuition for clean restaurants
with great food.
I loved listening to her smile as she told tales of their
vacations, travel conversations, and shopping finds.
I loved watching her unpin and re-pin her fine curly hair into
the styles she paired with her dress and sandals.
I loved how tickled she'd get when he'd call, send a card, or
chocolates.

I loved watching her twist the two engagement rings he'd
    given her as the jewels danced throughout time long
    after he'd gone.
I loved watching her strength and feeling empowered when
    she told me that she'd kept the rings but denied him
    marriage both times.
I loved to see her confidence radiate as she declared that
    she'd always be married to Johnson.
I loved dreaming about loving someone so much.
I loved hoping that I'd be married.
I loved wandering who my husband would be like. I loved
    thinking about loving with all the love I had to give.

Now that I'm older, with time moving forward,
My grandmother's stories of love are no more.
They'll always live with me. But I've had to write my own love
    stories
with the help of Sarah Dessen when trying to grow up.
The times are so different
And so are my stories
of love.

All while I was loving,
Sweet little ole me was ignoring the role of the male in a love
    story.
I loved listening to grandma's and being elated listening to
    her dreams and feelings.
Giggling that same giggle.

Everything I thought of love and wanted in love,
I lived through others' feelings.
Completely ignoring the importance of the male valuing me,
listening to me,
helping me mature.
I ignored understanding respect, self-worth, and faith.
I missed the point of the love stories.
I ignored learning that love isn't about what I wanted it to be.

Love is patient,
And it's kind,
It's slow to anger.
Love is genuine and sincere.
Love is sacrifice.

That's why she never remarried.

GRANDMOMMA

Strength comes with wisdom and
wisdom comes from experience.
My grandmomma was strong: Strong-minded, strong-witted,
     strong-willed and strong in faith.
That's how I know my grandmomma is fine.

Courage pairs with patience and
both look easy when done with grace.
My grandmomma embodied grace.

I saw it in her laugh, her smile, and
the way she'd cut her eyes. In knowing that,
I know my grandmomma is fine.
Kindness is an attribute that God blessed his angels with.
It's a trait that is shared with others through compassion.
My grandmomma was kind.
She taught me kindness with her compassion for others.
As long as I am kind and we are kind to each other.
I know my grandmomma is fine.
My grandmomma would always say, "I'm doing fine". She
     would never want her burdens to burden others;
     therefore, she gave her problems to God and left it at
     that.

I'm so grateful to God for allowing me to learn and grow
    from such a dynamic woman.
The stories I could tell you about my grandmomma could fill
    the public library twice.
We danced together; we laughed, cried, and stuck together.

My grandmomma understood me and I really knew her.
That's why all the tears I've shed are not from pain, anger,
or despair.
They are of joy.
I cry because my heart is now truly and eternally happy.
My grandmomma is my heart.
Because my heart beats strong
I know that she is fine.
My grandmomma loved flowers, the sunshine, a cool breeze,
    fellowship with good company,
to take quiet walks and have a good song to dance to.
My grandmomma smiled easily and loved wholly.

I take comfort in knowing she's walking around heaven,
dancing with the other angels, enjoying God's company,
Being proud of me
for knowing and telling everybody that...
"she is truly fine".

A TRAGEDY

Its a tragedy when men cheat.
when they cheat

they don't stop
and think
about the aftermath of their actions.

Selfish men
ignore the pain,
confusion, frustration, demolition of a family unit.

When a man cheats,
when he cheats
everyone
he loves feels his pain.

When men cheat
they stop thinking and
start seeking.

They seek a place to release.
They feel satisfaction
while
ignoring the truth.

Their decisions from the first touch are everlasting.

GRAMPA

She told me,
"Call him Daddy"
so I played along

even though

the one I called
Momma
assumed both roles.

The man I called grandaddy
is my mother's
not my own.

Granma never remarried
all of my life
her husband was gone.

Absent
vacant
murdered.

I call him Papa Johnson
because
he rolled like stones.

GROWING PAINS

I am no longer a child
yet
I am not quite a woman.

I am
exploring
falling
diving
deep into myself.

I am cascading into a river of possibilities.
As I am thrown against rock,
crashing,
I gain momentum
and press past pain.

Yielding only to the calm from seeking light
while
encapsulated by the abyss of possibility.

SEX

I know exactly what needs to be done.
I know exactly what to do
what needs to be omitted
and
everything to avoid.

Unfortunately,
I never take my own advice
or
think back on words I've shared with others.

'Sex is dangerous.

Proceed with caution.'

Until
it's Midnight
65 mph,
legs open to a night of passionate regrets.
Heart racing
body accelerating rapidly down emotions
Shame riddled highway until finally approaching
the stop sign at the intersection of
Round two and Cumtoyoursenses.

What the fuck just happened?
Panting to catch one's breath

BOOM
broken rubber
on the floor.

Hazard lights on.
Pull over to the shoulder and collect one's thoughts.
I'm pretty sure I've crashed.

FRIENDS WITH BENEFITS

We used to be friends
that all came to an end
abruptly.

Questions asked
no answers given
a multi-year friendship
ended.

There is no going back.

There are deep lessons in disagreements.

DEFINING FEELINGS

What the fuck is a title?

If I treat you kind
What the fuck is a title?

If I call you at night,
tell you the truth
when you're wrong or right?

Make you feel special
and remind you where I'm choosing
to spend my time.

What the fuck is a title?
Societal pressure
timelines and shit.

Why do I need to think about marriage or kids?
We are just fucking.

That's what I told myself
It is what it is
and
I don't want a title.

We were fucking;
Grown-up cuddling

somehow
we turned into friends.

GOD BLESS MY HUSBAND

I always ask the Lord to send me a good husband
because my dad wasn't hittin' on shit.

He didn't have a job for over 10 years,
And barely contributed
to
my future.

There were times when
I questioned my worth
and
whether or not I was worthy of anything
more than
nothing.
Because all my daddy had to give me was $20 and an opinion.
The opinion infinitely more often than
money.

My father set a good example of the kind of man
I should most certainly
avoid. I forgive him.

I know to run from deception
run
and not turn back.

To hide my smile behind tear-filled eyes and keep running
until my feet come off the ground and my life no longer
    confined
by earthly limits
and boundaries.

Trusting in my heavenly father
will forever keep me safe.

STEPMOTHER

Congratulations!
You have won.
Many women have fought and lost.

Countless hours of wasted time.
Years in a gauntlet of lies.
Guilt filled in restless nights
fore he could not do right by anyone.
Twenty-five years of those jaded, dark, bitter, broken eyes.

Wondering why he has wasted his potential,
never providing a return on his father's investments.
I pray GOD show you all mercy.
I pray that the man who loves me
does so selflessly

To make up for the selfishness of my father
and alter the view I have of man.
Whomever he has defined himself to you as.
Believe him.
Love him.
Celebrate my father because
you did it.
You've collected the ring.
You have won.

I hope you are it
and he can finally be happy
now.

DAD

Every time I seek forgiveness
genuinely scour the trenches of my soul
to forgive;

Purge myself of the hurt
rid every pore
cavity and crevice
within the entity of my essence
of the pain associated with the breath of a thought of you.

I call on Jesus
as I cower.

You are always forgiven.
I love you.

WOMAN

I've always been a girl
dreaming of being a lady.

Then, of course, I'll get married
become a wife and then a mommy.

Unfortunately,
I never saw myself as a woman.
I can't even define it.
I don't know what it means.
I can recognize it.

My mother,
a strong black woman,
raised me completely
alone.
I love her,
look up to her,
she is my hero.
We are not the same.

Me? I
am a girl?
Who,
owns a home,

a car,
and rental property.
I pay taxes and attention to salaries.
I can read,
drink,
ask questions,
and fuck.

In America,
that makes me
Woman.

LEG & LIQUOR STORE HOURS

It's 1 AM
and I am missing you.
Not you in the physical
your essence —

The conditions in which I had you.
Sexual paralysis
yours
mine
our
bodies

Connected
with trust
all while lacking commitment.

There is so much tension.
Every extension of my being
is completely longing
to be entangled in your arms.

REALITY CHECK

Young lady,
you ain't got it all.
You can't make shit happen.

YOU'RE NOT GOD.

Check yourself chile'
you're a wreck
apathetic, damn, motherfuckin mess.

Another man's hoe,
ole
would be babymama
Everybody knows the only reason you ain't one
is because you played the game smarter
— got birth control.

You are GROWN
Nobody is gonna fill your head with free loving.

Stop searching.

You know where the truth lies.
You are never alone.
You are wanted.

Especially when you feel like you don't belong.

Faith will always keep you strong.

HUSBAND

I made the acquaintance of a Cobb County resident,
living in Kansas at the time.
Crying over the pretty blonde girl that brought chaos into
       his life.

His name is biblical, familial, and
one I've been hearing since the womb was forming my ears.

A name, a person,
time will never let me forget.

I did not want to be a girlfriend,
I put in no demands for a relationship.
Intense pain would radiate in my core and brain
with any thought of it.

Subsequently,
I put myself in
cardiac arrest when
this man
I knew from a passed boyfriend
moved back home from Kansas.

Day one,
I thought

gorgeous,
tall,
dark hair
handsome.
2 years post-breakup
Hinge
reconnected us.

REASONS TO BREAKUP

In all my reflections
on this mess of a situation,
I realize the blame for my agony
frustration
and
pain
is not his
but
it is my own.

A four-month reconnection
turned into a lesson about
acceptance
settling
and
growth.

Before him,
I'd never been with a Virgo man.

There was a reason GOD sent this one to me.

He came back into my life right
before the start of the holiday season.
My first Christmas
as an orphan.

Every red flag, I ignored it.
I didn't want to be committed.
I opened myself to be disrespected.
Once permitted, the disrespect continued.

Why had I allowed it?
That has forever been on my mind.

My selfishness,
stress-induced carelessness,
my lust driven body
took refuge in his warmth.

Entangled in his bed,
every body part engaged in the spaces between our legs.

We
are
connected.

Surrendering our bodies to one another
Saturday after
Saturday Night.

Every moment passed without him
yielded anxious curiosity about future seconds with him.

As quick as a finger snap,
the foundation of the friendship

he and I were building collapsed.
In a series of slurry
a mindless outpouring
miscommunicated completely
based on his reaction when he heard
3 words.

I love you,
I love you.
I said it over and over.
A broken little girl in need of closeness.

Intimacy,
Genuine intimacy
I was aching,
begging
for my mother to rock me,
hold me,
hug me,
give me a kiss goodnight.

Instead,

the room spun and
he begged me to stop.
he asked me
Stop saying words that I didn't mean.
That's how I knew

his heart could love,
and maybe it wasn't holding any for me.

He didn't want me
I made myself an easy lay.
I gave him everything I had to offer
ignoring the role sex plays in love language.

I did not love him
I did not mean it how it was said.
Sure,
a drunken man will tell no tale
After morning and distance
I was sober.

I love him.
I love everyone.
I was raised to be Christian.

Was I genuinely in love with him??
Or
Did I love our friendship
and time together?

He was there to lend an ear whenever
I needed.
He made time for me.
He made sure I didn't feel lonely,

Or
orphaned.

He listened to understand
Stood strong as
comforter
confidant

I will always have love for him;
respect and appreciation.
Consequently,
the demise of our situationship
miscommunication
and
his family, friends,
and
associations
all preferred him to be with
An easier-to-digest woman.

He finds me good enough to fuck
but won't open his heart to love.
I'm welcome to be good to him
but the reciprocal,
I'm undeserving.

I listen to his farewell,
sobbing,

as he fumbles over why
We should stay broken up.

SCORN

There is never rest for the wicked.
For those without intention
especially when they say
they serve GOD

a GOD as deliberate as mine.

They will have no peace.

You wasted our time.
You proud arrogant bastard.
You wasted my time.
You selfish mealymouthed pauper.
You wasted Her time.

She's gone and we will never have those opportunities again.

We spent 14
fourteen months
hating each other. While you what?

Made marriage arrangements in a foreign land.

Was the "American" girl not good enough for the
person to his people who is innocent

who has done nothing.
When she was dying and we were all praying

were you praying her out of her misery and yours?

Did you speak to her every morning?
When did you speak again to her that night?
Did you beg your creator to get rid of her pain and her
     physical body
without feeling let down by you
the turmoil of you breaking her heart once again?
Too bad,
So sad
you let her down
But
She'd already let you go.

I was there to bear witness.

I pray GOD have mercy on you
May your soul be filled and saved by Christ's spirit.

The example you have set and the legacy you have left
are no more.

Fortunately for you,
where I was born,
I am what my father is.

The way you treated and left us
makes me black.

You being from Africa
made me African
So the world can label me African- American and charge me
    for my ancestor's reparations

but ultimately,
Life's experiences
Gave me the confidence to see love in being exactly who I am.

I am a
Black American.

MY SINGLE MOTHER WORKED FOR THE STATE

Six thirty
AM

taps on the door
Someone overslept.

She's nervous
but it's okay
'cause I'm gettin' up
to make sure she won't be late.

She's on bus duty
and those kids
just
don't act right.

I respect her commitment
and desire to be on time.

Two lessons I'll appreciate
every day of my life.

HONOR BY ACCEPTANCE

Momma,
Your compassion, your sacrifice, your essence
Has given me the courage
To be strong
achieve and pray
unceasingly
exceed my goals
simultaneously ignoring all limitations
Discerning love from hate
It brings me joy knowing that while you're up in heaven
I will be on earth being great.

TAKING CARE OF ELDERS

Out the front door
down the steps
across the yard
and jump over the ditch.

Head left up the road
another left at the fork
keep walking

Inez Watts must be outta town, it's quiet.

Look right
look left
double check then
hurry up and cross the street.

I'll sit on the swing
Granmama's going inside to see about her daddy.

SUMMER IN THE SOUTH

Sun shining,
It's up high and there ain't a cloud in sight.
Grass needs to be cut
and school is 3 weeks from over.

All that means is
summer is here!

The best ones come from Ingles.

It's all about the snap.

Red, green, purple, orange and blue juices
slip down the plastic tube.
Stickyin' up fingers, toes,
concrete
Doin' nothing really but
stainin' clothes.

Freeze it, melt it, eat it
soon as she'd buy them,
they were gone.

One for after breakfast,
one before lunch

another cuz it's so hot
then 1 more because,
why not?

Gotta grab one for Granma
better make that two,
just in case she don't wanna eat alone.

Eating one more after dinner
got my last one with
a kiss goodnight.

Popsicles are my sweetest memories from childhood
    summertime.

MY BODY IS MINE

Sticks insert themselves wherever they're able to fit.
Upon any whim

Your undue burden will not burden me.
A burden,
my burden

The burden
of looking at a life brought into this world
and thinking

"maybe I should have gotten an abortion?"

CONFESSING AND REPENTING

To repent is to confess,
to confess is to release
to release is to trust
to trust is to know
that you are never going to know it all.
You have done nothing.
You own nothing.
You are nothing without GOD.

You are loved by GOD
more than man's capacity,
that is why man is nothing but energetic entities within a
        physical realm.
Man messes up.

Jesus, the most beloved sacrifice, saves.

You are saved by his blood
feel his grace every day in all that is good.
Misery is chosen
nothing from GOD is miserable.
Man makes choices for mankind.

GOD created man,
therefore seek and trust GOD

not man.
Love man, be kind to man, forgive.

To forgive is to realize all mankind makes mistakes.
Listen to an apology
for an apology is a confession.

Repentance,
Acknowledgment of mistake,
wrong choice,
Misjudgment,
deceit,
betrayal,
neglect,

self-righteousness,
and indignation,
arrogance.
I beg you,
repent.

ROMANCE

The huge wave of emotion
Catches by surprise.
Overcoming body
drowning mind
leaving being incapacitated.

Romance feels antiquated.
Long gone are the days were women
wait
with patience and prudence
for that man to ask her to dance.

Take her hand
glide her across the floor
spinning her heart into
dizzied memories love, forever, and
family.

White dresses, picket fences
virginity and obedience
a homemaker
— subordinate.

Today's woman creates her own choices.
No means

no relations with employers or husbands.
Her body is hers.
She no longer wants to stay virgin.
She knows good dick and finds pleasure in its poison.
Forbidden fruit attached to some dude
who ain't shit.
Reason ignored.

While the cowardice within the beholder of devil dick,
grooms,
brainwashes and leaves the woman powerless
And forced to actualize familial curses of lovelessness.

Romance.

HEAVY BLEEDING

I've never wanted to be a stick.
I'm grateful that I bleed.
Sticks will never know

Strength.

Although they have the abilities
To stick and leave,
To conquer, possess, and dictate.
Yet still, they are afraid of pain.

They possess power and have no strength
To be able to bleed
You have to be
okay with never

being
As good as
Pretty
As deserving as
Those created equally

Different.

I've never wanted to be a stick because

Bleeders bleed and
Breed resilience.
Any old body can be a dick.

RESISTANCE

I don't feel like it
so I'm not
smiling.

I don't feel like getting to know you
or
remembering how we met.

Don't feel like any of it.

LOVE IS AN ACTION VERB.

Love is an action verb.

Not just some word, said without expectation.

You call me
Question how I'm doing
Then leave the call abruptly satisfied with a half-hearted
    response.

Love is more than flamboyant recognition or praise;
more honest than public displays
sturdier than the blood rushing through our veins

It is not defined by its entanglement or activity
with familial bonds.

FUCKED UP FAMILY

16
when her brother died.
His choice changed her life.

Detaching and fastening knots to secure
strong healthy family ties.
Away to the wilderness
she was sent

Just 16,
when in 2017—he overdosed

SCHEDULE 1-4

EVERYTIME I take it,
I forget.
The shitty parts
All I remember is the good.

After the water is swallowed
The pledge is sure to follow
Along with regret.

Some say the trick is to
Live beneath the influence.
Above it is just
Stagnant decline in quality of living
A life
Void of feeling.

Sadness, pain, emotions
Consequence of the comedown
All Reasons— behind the chase.

FAMILY, LIFE'S FIRST TEACHER

Family is the best teacher.
Thanks to them,
life's lessons are learned earlier.

Bruises heal quicker,
The body's system becomes immune
to hatred from
unneeded friends

Full of silent targeted
rage.

RECONCILING WITH THE PAST

Fly,

I close my eyes to see you.
In and out of consciousness,
REM
and you're right there
elegant
beautiful
erect
regal.

Clearly,
YOU are an angel.

REFLECTIONS FROM TENNESSEE

As water rushes over rock,
Earth's quiet still transports
my thinking to a different time.

A fly landed on my notebook
as I was trying to write
about a hike
through Tennessee's Mountains.

The hum of rushing water
as it bumps against rock.
Yellow, butterfly hop along
dancing.

BEACHES OF GRIEF

Intertwined legs pressed firmly against mattress
soft feminine fingers,
long glittering nails,
interlock rough, callous knuckles

Reality becomes landscape.

Pale blues, pure white, bright green
the sun;
Floating within new found freedom,
I desperately search for something
someone I can tether myself to fill your void.

Actively combating
passively avoiding
feelings,
emotions. memories.
Lost at sea,
my body is beaten.

My skin is tattered
Consequence of earth's relentless gravitational pull.

Tides, currents, rocks
crashing
grief.

GHOST

Will you tuck me in tonight?
Brush your fingers across my hair
Rock me to sleep while softly kissing my forehead?

If not in a picture, I can only see you in my dreams.
Your body no longer exists in this realm;
you're no longer physically with me.
I beg you.
Come back.
If only while I'm sleeping.

Tuck me in and brush my hair
Hug me, hold me,
Reassure me of your love.
Your pride in my accomplishments

Oh how I miss the softness in your hands and the tickle of
     your fingertips on my shoulder.
Hopefully, the yearning subsides
When I become older... and have babies of my own.

For now, in my current state, you, the focus of my reverie
     while I'm awake.
By day's end, after kneeling down to pray
I crawl into bed and plead with GOD
for your arms to be outstretched, waiting for me in my
     dreams.

RIGHT TO REFUSE

My great-grandmother was born into love.
she experienced the earth.
But war and disruption
caused trouble and interrupted that freedom.

Everyone else in my family
has been born into hatred.
I refuse;

to bring a child into this world.

A world of hate,
that
prioritizes
larceny
dishonesty
oppression.

My child will NOT be a nigger,
spick, chink, or coon.
I genuinely refuse.

If I have to be a revolutionary,
then that is how they will address me.
For, I want to be a mother in this life

and that means changing this world is

A necessity. American Politics

I don't think Jesus was white,
but I know
he is real.

I know the peace and love only he can give.
Call me stupid,
call me crazy
tell me I'm running from truth.
I believe in Jesus because my life is not lived by you.

You are living your life
and traveling along your path.
Everything you have
experienced is yours and solely that.

I appreciate your kindness and genuine
openness to share your gifts and talent with me.
I've learned there is more to GOD than Christianity.

I've learned to inquire about my people.
I've learned of my people's ancient religions.
I've learned that man took power
and connected it to souls.

That was wrong.
Generations disconnected from ancestors
Dying in the wilderness
while calling America
home.

That doesn't make the facts any less
true.
Jesus is real.

He is a friend.
I know him well.
He has held me when I could no longer
stand to step.

As I continue to learn more
about
my power and self.
I know Jesus will be with me when there is no one else.

CREATED BEING

Stop acting like you don't know
his name!
Stop looking, seeking, pleasing man.

Shit will get you in trouble every time.
Passing around pussy
like a drunk bitch in a frat house.

Unconsciously,
doing things to be everything other than rejected.
You've already been forgiven and accepted by the King
Your Father,
the most high.

Just as you are.
He will purify your heart
and
remake your whole.
He will tend the cracks in your foundation.
Craters you created.

Carelessly,
begging randoms into your temple
letting them take your peace
and leave cum stains on your soul.

All in avoidance of physically being alone?

Girl,
grow up!
You are not a child in this world.
You've lived just about a year without your mom.
You gotta live some more.
Renew your faith in the lord.

Do not go astray.
Your foundation was set upon rock
it will not easily wash away.

Self-destructive tendencies
stemming from insecurities about what you lack
self-hatred because GOD made you
BLACK.

A deconstructed house, rubble, atop solid ground.

Remember what you know.

Stop forgetting your heavenly father's hand is there
leading you forward
Jesus has your back.

Jesus specializes in fixing broken houses,

a carpenter
is what he was when his feet made prints on the ground.
An expert in construction.
his occupation,
building houses.

Our creator's word
the ground
your house is built on.
The love of GOD will sustain it.
GOD alone turns houses into home.

Stop running away from what you know in search of what
you don't.

FREEDOM TO BE FREE

No need to prove anything,
not even your strength.

Seek adventure
Broaden your horizons
explore without restraint.

You were born who you are.
No need to question from angst.

So what if you're a woman?

Learn how to be one with the eyes,
ears,
and heart.

Trust in your creator.

Know GOD.

ACKNOWLEDGEMENTS

THANK YOU FOR reading. I give special thanks to my father, a great friend to my mother. I would also like to thank my uncles, aunts, and cousins who pushed me to keep going and be happy. I would like to thank my friends who have taken root in my heart. You have become family.

Huge thanks to those I love who are no longer a part of my life. You are forgiven and appreciated. Thank you Telor for being the amazing friend my mother said you'd be. You're brilliant. Thank you Cassidy for always being there. You are a blessed presence in my life.

I'd like to thank Mineset Bitcoin, Max Keiser, Isaiah Jackson, Jack Mallers and the team at Strike, The Bitcoin & Lightning Devs, The Bitcoin Beach team, The Remnant, and the Plebs on Bitcoin Twitter for my orange pill, their hard work, amazing memes, and wit that kept me chuckling down the rabbit hole.

Finally, I'd like to thank Stanford, media extraordinaire. Your friendship, perspective, and ability to understand my vision is a true show of your character. You take such amazing photos same as every other skill and talent you've been blessed with. You are appreciated. Stanford Davis (@stanthecamman) donated his images simply to add dynamism to my work. I am beyond grateful. If you appreciate his work and would like to support Stanford's art, feel free to scan the QR code and tip him sats. The address is to a wallet he holds the keys to. Donating sats to an artist is an amazing way to test out sending sats before you move large amounts *off the exchange* into your hardware wallet.

bc1qzm7d7npgnkezh05th38vul2x4l4a35y2x0fju6

WORKS CITED

Ajiboye, Timi, et al. *The Little Bitcoin Book: Why Bitcoin Matters for Your Freedom, Finances, and Future.* 21 Million Books, 2019.

Anderson, Claud. *A Black History Reader: 101 Questions You Never Thought to Ask.* PowerNomics, 2017.

Anderson, Claud. *Black Labor, White Wealth: The Search for Power and Economic Justice.* PowerNomics Corporation of America Publisher, 1994.

Anderson, Claud. *PowerNomics®: The National Plan to Empower Black America.* PowerNomics Corp. of America, 2001.

Atinuke, and Mouni Feddag. *Africa, Amazing Africa.* Candlewick Press, 2021.

Baradaran, Mehrsa. *The Color of Money: Black Banks and the Racial Wealth Gap.* The Belknap Press of Harvard University Press, 2019.

Booth, Jeff. *The Price of Tomorrow: Why Deflation Is the Key to an Abundant Future.* Stanley Press, 2020.

Breedlove, Robert, et al. *Thank God for Bitcoin: The Creation, Corruption and Redemption of Money.* Bitcoin and Bible Group, 2020.

Gigi, Der. *21 Lessons: What I've Learned from Falling down the Bitcoin Rabbit Hole.* Verlag Nicht Ermittelbar, 2019.

Green, Toby. *A Fistful of Shells: West Africa from the Rise of the Slave Trade to the Age of Revolution.* The University of Chicago Press, 2021.

Griffin, G. Edward. *The Creature from Jekyll Island: A Second Look at the Federal Reserve.* American Media, 2010.

Jackson, John G., et al. *Introduction to African Civilizations.* Citadel Press, 2001.

Williams, Jason. *Bitcoin: Hard Money You Can't F*Ck With: Why Bitcoin Will Be the next Global Reserve Currency.* Going Parabolic Publishing, 2020.

Woodson, Carter Godwin. *The Mis-Education of the Negro.* Tate, 2020.

ABOUT THE AUTHOR

Dope vibe
havin'
Bitcoin'n
black southern lady who chooses to love the Lord more than
  anything
in and of
the world.

P ASSIONATE ABOUT BITCOIN and in love with who GOD created,
A. Centauri graduated college with a Bachelor's of Science
in Integrated Studies focusing on Biological Sciences and a
Minor in Dance. She spends her free-time dancing, exercising,
reading, and discovering history's hidden truths. Inspired by
the teachings of Dr. Claud Anderson, Dr. Carter G. Woodson,
and Mehrsa Baradaran, A. Centauri uncovered a hidden
truth about Black America that compelled her to write about
her findings.

A lover of outdoor adventure, when she is not hiking with
her family she can be found gardening, visiting friends and

markets, and evangelizing about Bitcoin with strangers. She really believes Bitcoin fixes the money problem and therefore fixes the world she wants to bring children into.

The quest for truth has also led the author down a private unconventional way of living. She can be found on Twitter learning about Bitcoin, naturopathy, cattle farms, and lightning nodes.

www.ingramcontent.com/pod-product-compliance
Lightning Source LLC
Chambersburg PA
CBHW071201210326
41597CB00016B/1627